W9-COS-587

THE JAPANESE AMERICAN
FAMILY
ALBUM

THE JAPANESE AMERICAN
FAMILY
ALBUM

DOROTHY AND THOMAS HOOBLER
Introduction by George Takei

OXFORD UNIVERSITY PRESS • NEW YORK • OXFORD

Authors' Note

In Japan, a person's name is customarily written with the family name first.
In some of the first-person accounts in this book, Japanese Americans follow
that practice, too. Elsewhere, however, we have followed the American style
of writing the family name last and personal name first.

Oxford University Press

Oxford New York
Athens Auckland Bangkok Bombay
Calcutta Cape Town Dar es Salaam Delhi
Florence Hong Kong Istanbul Karachi
Kuala Lumpur Madras Madrid Melbourne
Mexico City Nairobi Paris Singapore
Taipei Tokyo Toronto

and associated companies in
Berlin Ibadan

Design: Sandy Kaufman
Layout: Greg Wozney
Consultant: Brian Niiya, collection manager, Japanese American National Museum in Los Angeles, California

Published by Oxford University Press, Inc.,
198 Madison Avenue, New York, New York 10016

Oxford is a registered trademark of Oxford University Press

Library of Congress Cataloging-in-Publication Data

Hoobler, Dorothy.
The Japanese American family album / Dorothy and Thomas Hoobler.
p. cm. — (American family albums)
Includes bibliographical references and index.
1. Japanese American families—Juvenile literature.
I. Hoobler, Thomas. II. Title. III. Series.
E184.J3H584   1995
306.8'089956073—dc20   94-43466
                                              CIP
                                              AC

ISBN 0-19-508131-5 (lib. ed.); ISBN 0-19-509934-6 (trade ed.); ISBN 0-19-510172-3 (series, lib. ed.)

1 3 5 7 9 8 6 4 2

Printed in the United States of America
on acid-free paper

Cover: The Hashimoto family in Baldwin Park, near Los Angeles, 1924.

Frontispiece: Issei, or first-generation, parents with their Nisei, or second-generation, children in Idaho in 1907.

Contents page: A Japanese American woman in Hawaii around 1910 carries her baby while she works.

CONTENTS

Takei's mother (the girl standing) with her family in Florin, California. Her parents—her father is standing and her mother is seated—immigrated to the United States around 1900.

George Takei is a television, film, and stage actor who is probably best known for his role as Mr. Sulu in the TV series "Star Trek." His film credits include starring roles in the British film Return from the River Kwai *and the Australian film* Prisoners of the Sun.

In 1988, Takei received a Grammy nomination in the category of Best Spoken Word Recording; his distinctive voice has been featured in numerous "Star Trek" audio novel recordings. He has also been a guest voice on the TV show "The Simpsons."

In addition to his achievements in the entertainment industry, Takei is a community activist in his native Los Angeles. He has served on the boards of many local civic and cultural groups, including the Friends of Little Tokyo Arts and the El Pueblo Park Association. He is also on the board of the Japanese American National Museum, the Los Angeles Theatre Center, and the Los Angeles Conservancy.

In 1991, George Takei placed his signature and handprint in the forecourt of Mann's Chinese Theatre in Hollywood. His autobiography, To the Stars, *was published in 1994.*

George Takei (holding a comic book), his brother Henry, sister Nancy, and parents, Emily and Takekuma, in Los Angeles in 1942, just before they were interned.

Takei (at left) with his mother, brother, and sister at Camp Tule Lake, California. Takei spent much of his childhood in the internment camps.

Takei, as Commander Sulu, at the helm of the starship Enterprise *in* Star Trek II: The Wrath of Khan. *At left is Kirstie Alley as Lieutenant Saavik, at the back is Leonard Nimoy as Captain Spock, and at right is William Shatner as Admiral Kirk.*

INTRODUCTION

by George Takei

"The greatness of America," my father used to say, "is that this country is a government of the people." But he always followed that with, "The weakness of America is that it's as fallible as people. America is so dependent on good people being part of the process."

When my grandparents made the ocean journey from Japan to California around the turn of the century, they brought with them the drive, ambitions, and dreams of all immigrants. But America was not a hospitable land to them. Their labor was needed, but they were harshly received. Unlike other immigrants, the Japanese were prohibited from becoming naturalized citizens. By law, they were forbidden to own land. Their children's education was segregated and inferior.

Despite these adversities, my maternal grandparents, Benkichi and Shigeno Nakamura, went into the Sacramento delta and worked what was then wasteland. Their toil turned that neglected spread of dirt into rich farmland, contributing to the development of agribusiness, a major sector of the California economy today. Yet they could not own the farm they developed. There, in 1912, my mother was born.

My paternal grandfather, Yataro Takei, was a widower with two young sons when he went to San Francisco in 1915 to build a new life. One of the boys, then 13 years old, was my father. Grandfather Takei, undaunted by the antagonisms of this country, threw himself into the life of his new Japantown community. He got a job with the local Japanese news-paper, *Nichibei Shimbun,* chronicling the daily life of the immigrants. And he worked to educate his sons, eventually seeing my father graduate from business college.

It was in the booming city of Los Angeles that my father, Takekuma Takei, met my mother, Emily. They were married on the 27th floor of the landmark City Hall. By the time I was born, they had a successful dry cleaning business in the Wilshire district. Things were going well. Then Pearl Harbor was bombed and everything changed cataclysmically.

Young Japanese American men who volunteered at army recruitment offices were summarily rejected, classified 4C—the same as enemy aliens. In the war hysteria, Americans could not draw the distinction between U.S. citizens of Japanese ancestry and the imperial Japanese military we were fighting. The fundamental American ideal of due process vanished. Although no criminal charges were filed and no trials were held, Japanese Americans on the West Coast were forcibly put into internment camps. Armed soldiers came to our home and took us to the horse stables at Santa Anita race track, then to Camp Rohwer in the swamps of Arkansas. A year later, we were moved to another camp at Tule Lake in cold and windy northern California.

Yet even behind the barbed-wire fence of internment camps, my father struggled to help sustain the community. At both camps, he worked as the block manager. My mother worked to make a home for us in tar-paper barracks. I began kindergarten at Camp Rohwer, not understanding the irony of my pledging allegiance to the American flag every morning. However, the young Japanese American men who volunteered for the military, and this time were taken because of the manpower shortage, fully felt the sharp poignancy of donning the same uniform as that of the guards that watched over their families. These men, placed in segregated outfits—the 442nd Regimental Combat Team and the Military Intelligence Service—served with extraordinary valor. The 442nd became one of the most decorated units of World War II.

There were other young men, standing on principle, who refused to serve while their families were in barbed-wire incarceration. For this audacious stand, they were locked up in Leavenworth Federal Penitentiary. These men, too, are American heroes. Whether by the blood shed by the 442nd or by the hard time done in federal prison, their courage added new dimensions to the meaning of being American. The fidelity to ideals and the patriotism of these men paved the way for Congress to pass legislation in 1952 that at long last granted naturalized citizenship to Asian immigrants.

After 37 years in this country, my father, then 50 years old, was able to sign up to become an American. "This country is a participatory democracy," he said. "I want to be a participant helping keep America closer to its ideals." He understood profoundly the value of his citizenship because he knew the price that had been paid for it.

George Takei

A family in Japan before they emigrated to California around 1910.

CHAPTER ONE

THE OLD COUNTRY

O n July 8, 1853, four large black ships appeared off the coast of Japan. The first people to see the vessels thought that two of them must be on fire. They were steamships, giving off clouds of smoke—something that most Japanese had never seen before. That was only the first of the surprises that Commodore Matthew C. Perry of the United States Navy brought to Japan.

At the time Perry's ships arrived, Japan had been virtually isolated from the rest of the world for 250 years. About once a year, a Dutch merchant ship docked at the Japanese port of Deshima to carry on limited trade. Aside from that, Japan was closed to foreigners, and no Japanese was allowed to leave the country.

With the exception of a few scholars who read books brought by the Dutch, the Japanese people were ignorant of the developments that had been made in science and technology since 1600 in Europe and America. Thus, when Commodore Perry fired his ships' cannons—merely as a demonstration—the Japanese were awed.

Perry had brought a letter from the President of the United States, Millard Fillmore. It asked permission for American ships to stop at Japanese ports to take on supplies. Fillmore also suggested that both countries might benefit from trading with one another. After delivering the message to the local governor, Perry departed. He promised to return in a year to receive the reply.

This brief visit initiated an upheaval that permanently changed Japan. At the time, Japanese society was strictly divided into four classes of people. At the bottom were merchants; above them, in ascending order, were artisans, farmers, and *samurai*, or warriors. The Japanese emperor, who lived in the city of Kyoto, carried out certain religious duties on behalf of the people. Real power, however, rested in the hands of the *shogun*, or military leader. In 1603, a samurai named Ieyasu Tokugawa had defeated the last of his enemies at the battle of Sekigahara. Since then, the title of shogun had been passed on to Tokugawa's descendants, who lived in Edo (today's Tokyo).

As news of Perry's visit spread, many Japanese determined to resist the demands of this new "barbarian" visitor, the Americans. The small island nation had faced foreign invaders before and had always defeated them. Six centuries earlier, the Mongols—whose mounted warriors had spread across Asia and into Europe—had tried to land an army on Japan. But a typhoon had arrived just in time to sink the Mongol fleet. To the Japanese this "divine wind," or *kamikaze*, was a sign that Japan was a land blessed and protected by the gods.

However, the Tokugawa shogun had better information than his subjects about the military power of the United States and Europe. Just 11 years before, warships from Great Britain had bombarded China, Japan's huge mainland neighbor, and forced the Chinese emperor to accept British demands for colonies and trade. Thus, when Perry returned in 1854, the shogun signed a treaty that granted the relatively modest American proposals.

Many Japanese *daimyos*, hereditary nobles and large landholders of the samurai class, were enraged by what they regarded as the shogun's humiliating surrender. Rallying around the only possible rival to the shogun—the emperor himself—they started a rebellion. The last of the Tokugawa shoguns resigned in 1868. The emperor, as a sign of his new political power, moved into the shogun's old castle in Edo, and the city was renamed Tokyo, or "eastern capital."

The emperor was a 15-year-old boy named Mutsuhito. As was the custom, he adopted a name for his reign: Meiji ("illustrious rule"). The Meiji Restoration, in which power was restored to the emperor after centuries of military rule, marks the beginning of Japan's modern history.

The young emperor's advisers promptly decided that the shogun's policy toward the "barbarians" was not wrong after all. Indeed, they carried it much farther than the shogun would have dared to go. Meiji's advisers recognized that if Japan was to avoid being colonized by European nations—as other Asian countries had been—it must quickly become as powerful as they were. To do that, Japan should modernize by adopting the best features of the Western countries. Japanese students soon traveled to the United States and Europe to learn about Western science, forms of government, and military skills.

Adaptation of the cultural features of other countries was nothing new to the Japanese. Until the 7th century, the Japanese had no written language; then, they adopted the characters of the Chinese language to write Japanese. The ideas of Confucius, an ancient Chinese philosopher, strongly influenced Japanese society, too. The Confucian ideals include respect for superiors, devotion to duty, and family loyalty—all of which became as distinctive a feature of Japanese society as they were in China.

Japanese society was based on a delicate web of relationships. Each person knew his or her place in the social structure and accepted certain duties toward others. *Giri*, for instance, was the obligation owed to someone who had done a favor or provided gifts, goods, or services. *Enryo* was the respect owed to superiors; it determined proper conduct in all ordinary relation-

A Japanese family in Kobe in 1938. The inscription on the back of the photograph gives the year as "Showa 12." This meant the 12th year of the reign of the Showa emperor, who took the throne at the end of 1926.

ships. *Enryo* might also be translated as "polite restraint." In practice, *enryo* meant not to demand or expect too much from another person, so that the relationship is not strained. *On* was the deepest form of obligation—it implied a debt that can never be repaid. Children owed *on* to their parents and ancestors, who gave them life.

Two religions have had particular influence in Japanese culture: Shinto and Buddhism. Shinto is the ancient Japanese religion of nature worship. Its adherents believe that *kami*, or spirits, inhabit many natu-

ral objects, from stones to trees to waterfalls. Making offerings to ancestors is part of Shinto, for the *kami* of deceased ancestors provide help to their descendants. Yet most Japanese also practice Buddhism. Buddhist ceremonies are held for important changes in life—births, marriages, and deaths. Some men and women enter Buddhist monasteries, seeking a life of prayer and contemplation.

One great change that the officials of the Meiji Restoration brought about was to dismantle the feudal system that had existed in Japan for centuries. The *daimyos* lost their lands, which were distributed to the farmers who lived on them. The samurai were stripped of their privileges, and Japan built its new military forces by drafting the sons of farmers.

Japan showed that it had learned its military lessons well by defeating the larger but far weaker Chinese Empire in the Sino-Japanese War of 1894–95. Ten years later, the Japanese scored an even more stunning victory over the Russian Empire. It was the first time an Asian nation had ever defeated a European power. These triumphs brought enormous prestige to Japan's military leadership.

The Meiji emperor died in 1912 and was succeeded by his eldest son, Yoshihito. Afflicted by mental illness, Yoshihito was a weak ruler. By the time his own son, Hirohito, ascended to the throne in 1926, the emperor's role had become that of a figurehead. Civilian and military officials made all the government decisions.

Hirohito took for his reign the name Showa, meaning "enlightened peace." The name would ring hollow in the years that followed, however, as the increasingly militaristic Japanese government adopted an aggressive foreign policy that would lead to the nation's involvement in World War II.

Meanwhile, Japan's growing might had not brought a better life to all of its people. Though the farmers now owned their land, they had to pay an annual tax to the government. This tax remained the same regardless of the size of the harvest. Overpopulation and natural disasters caused poverty and hunger in some Japanese farming regions. In 1884, the *Japan Weekly Mail* reported that "although crops were good the years before, the poor of the nation did not have enough to eat.... Some starved to death.... Some existed on tree barks and roots."

To help resolve the situation, in 1886 the Japanese government passed a law that allowed its citizens to emigrate. The law was regarded as a modern adaptation of the traditional practice of *dekasegi*, whereby Japanese left their native villages in hard times to find work elsewhere in the nation.

The first Japanese overseas emigrants went to Hawaii, which was then an independent kingdom. Americans who had established sugar plantations in the Hawaiian Islands sent labor contractors to recruit Japanese farmers. It was not hard to persuade them to sign contracts, for the wages were high compared to those in Japan. One emigrant calculated that in a year overseas he could save almost 1,000 yen—the annual salary for the governor of a Japanese prefecture, or province.

In 1923, Shigezo Iwata, at left, with other members of his kendo *(wooden-sword fighting)* class at Waseda University. The kendo *master is seated in front. Iwata emigrated to the United States the next year.*

At about the same time, Japanese began to emigrate to the United States. These first-generation immigrants were called *Issei,* which comes from the Japanese word for "one." Their images of America had been formed by popular guidebooks, with titles such as *Mysterious America* and *Come, Japanese!* Many of the guidebooks presented an overly optimistic picture of what the emigrants would find. One claimed, "Gold, silver, and gems are scattered on [the] streets. If you can figure out a way of picking them up, you'll become rich instantly."

Most of the early immigrants were sojourners: individuals who left Japan with the intention of making enough money to return home prosperous. Japanese newspapers printed numerous accounts of those who had succeeded in doing so, setting off a wave of "emigration fever."

For similar reasons, some Japanese families borrowed money to send their male children to the United States to get an education. A 1906 issue of the Japanese publication *America-Bound Magazine* contained an article entitled "How to Graduate from College without a Penny." But in the United States, many of these ambitious students learned the truth. Few actually entered college, instead taking jobs as servants or laborers to earn the money to repay their families for the cost of their ship tickets.

Finally, some young men went to the United States to evade Japan's military draft, which claimed men between the ages of 17 and 40 for service in the army and navy. A family could protect one son from the draft by naming him the heir to its land. It was a Japanese custom for only one son to inherit the family farm. As a result, many "second sons" chose to seek their fortunes overseas.

Like immigrants from all nations, the Japanese arrived in the United States with the hope of making a better life for themselves. Their experiences, however, were often far different from what they had expected.

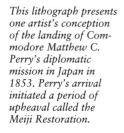

Most Japanese immigrants to Hawaii and the United States came from Honshu, the largest of Japan's islands. After 1900, numerous immigrants from Okinawa also began arriving in Hawaii.

LIFE IN JAPAN

Toru Matsumoto, born on Hokkaido, the northernmost of Japan's four major islands, emigrated to the United States in the 1920s. He recalled how the arrival of Commodore Perry's ships affected his samurai grandfather.

Grandmother's late husband had been a warrior. In the last days of the Tokugawa shogunate, he fell in love with Kiyo, who was the daughter of a local war lord. At that time, the right of choosing to marry for love was confined to a privileged few among the Japanese aristocracy. Ordinarily, my grandfather would have had no hope for the realization of his desire. But just then the shogun government was on the point of crumbling, following the surprise visit of Commander Perry. How amazed Perry would have been to know that his visit played a part in the romance of a Japanese warrior and his bride!

Perry came in 1853, with four black warships, demanding the opening of the country for trade. The shogun government tottered. Four battleships with guns! Japan possessed only small fishing boats and freight boats.... On Perry's return in 1854 the treaties were signed.

The whole country was thrown into chaos which lasted 14 years, until in 1867 the last shogun surrendered his authority to the royal family.

My grandfather saw the signs of the times. He deserted the war lord, who was a subject of the shogun, and eloped with my grandmother. In normal times the young couple would have been searched out and punished for their elopement, but now they were forgotten. They emerged from the revolution to live an inconspicuous but happy life.

This lithograph presents one artist's conception of the landing of Commodore Matthew C. Perry's diplomatic mission in Japan in 1853. Perry's arrival initiated a period of upheaval called the Meiji Restoration.

Matsumoto described his childhood memories of his grandmother.

Father's mother, my grandmother Kiyo, lived with us. She and I became fast friends. Her hair was gray, and her face full of wrinkles like a dried plum. She called me "Toru, Toru," and she loved me.

She was small, and her back was slightly bent. But that back was my main means of transportation, for she carried me everywhere on it, except in winter, when she stayed indoors. As soon as the sun had melted the winter's snow, she would carry me to the corner candy store where she bought me "drops." They were black drops, the size of a large marble, made of brown sugar. Five of them cost one sen. I put one in one cheek, another one in the other. I kept them in my mouth a long time while carrying the other three in a bag.

Mother did not approve. It was not good for my health to eat between meals, and besides, the candy drops might make my teeth decay.

When Grandmother was not walking with me, she would sit in front of the family Buddhist sanctuary and recite the liturgy for hours. She would light the candles, open the two small doors to reveal the golden image of Buddha, and clap her hands several times as she bowed piously. Every morning, as soon as breakfast was cooked, she would put the newly cooked rice and soybean soup in front of the sanctuary before she herself would sit down at the breakfast table. This was done in the belief that the spirits of her ancestors needed food on their long journey to Paradise. When she was not busy with her acts of piety toward her Buddha, she was either scolding her daughter-in-law [a Christian] or denouncing the "pagan" religion which this daughter-in-law brought with her.

Grandmother was interesting even to a young child like me because her teeth were dyed completely black. I learned when I grew older that a faithful widow followed this custom in Japan to make herself unattractive to other men in order to show her fidelity to her dead husband.

Kihachi Hirakawa was born in the town of Matsudo, 10 miles from Tokyo. An early emigrant to the United States, he described his life in Japan in his autobiography.

I was born in a well-known family...in the year, 1864. My parents were Mr. and Mrs. Tomigoro Hirakawa. The Hirakawas had been in the brewing business, making sake [Japanese rice wine], for many generations. My mother's maiden name was Maki Masuda, and the Masuda family, who lived twelve miles from our town, were brewers, too.

Until a century ago our families were rich people, but my father failed in business, calamity, unhappiness followed the loss of much money, so as a consequence, my father gave up his business.

What was my father's next venture? He decided to be a

Natural calamities such as a drought in 1883 and a major storm in southern Japan in 1884 caused an economic depression and widespread suffering. In the summer of 1885, a Yamaguchi newspaper reporter wrote:

The depression has gotten worse in every village, town, and district. But what strikes me most is the hardships paupers are having in surviving. The worse-off people are the fishermen and farmers....Their regular fare consists of rice husk or buckwheat chaff ground into powder and the dregs of bean curd mixed with leaves and grass.

Members of the first Japanese diplomatic mission to the United States in 1860. The two swords that the men wear indicate their status as samurai, members of the hereditary warrior class.

Japanese women feed mulberry leaves to silkworms, which spin silk to construct their cocoons during the caterpillar stage. Later, workers will carefully unwind these cocoons to harvest the fine thread used to make silk cloth.

The Fujiwara family hunts for mushrooms near Osaka in 1902. Shiitake mushrooms, brown and more flavorful than the white kind sold in American supermarkets, are used extensively in Japanese cooking.

rice-merchant instead of a brewer, but when fortune did not come in ten years, he gave up his new enterprise, left our native place, and moved to Tokyo, the fifth year of Meiji in 1872 when I was eight years old.

When our family moved from my native town Matsudo to the city of Tokyo, we numbered eight; my parents, my brother, three sisters, and my grandfather. How do you think we traveled? No, not by a streamlined car, nor by truck, nor on foot but on a rice boat. This boat carried rice from place to place along the river. We took not only all our belongings with us on the boat, but also many provisions.

At last we reached our destination, the home of my grandfather's nephew...in the eastern part of the city. My father wished to continue in the rice business so he found a store in...the northern part of the city....

It was at the end of this year, Dec. 30, 1872, that a dreadful disaster took place. I can hear those terrible fire bells ringing even yet in my memory; ringing from every bell-tower. A strong west wind was blowing, and soon the fire spread over several blocks, and after several hours had elapsed, 3,000 houses were burned. Our new store was one that was destroyed, and with it our furniture, clothing, and rice were all lost.

I shall never forget my mother's tears at this catastrophe.

Osame Nagata Manago, who left Japan for Hawaii in 1913, was born in 1895 in Fukuoka prefecture. When she was 85, she described how she and her four sisters worked hard in the fields during the rice season in Japan:

We made good rice. In our time, in Fukuoka-*ken* [*ken* means prefecture], we would plant rice seedlings one by one along ropes which were set from one end of the field to the other. When we had five people working together, we had five rows being planted at the same time. And the field had to look neat horizontally, vertically, and diagonally. Finishing one line, we went on to the next, after measuring it correctly. When we came to the end of the field, the work was completed.

After four weeks or so, the seedlings which had looked so fragile would settle more securely in the soil. Then we had to weed. If people did not work hard, the grass grew tall. Since there weren't any chemicals to kill weeds like nowadays, we had to weed by hand and soon lost our fingernails.

And in those days, we had a horse. We used to spread its dung on thick straw mats, and dry it for manure in the field. We also used human feces. Not now, but in those days, we used it as a fertilizer. We would buy and carry it in a cart. We called it *shirimochi*: *shiri* for "buttocks" and *mochi* for "rice cakes." We took people some rice in return for the manure.

Then after three to four weeks, the ground got hard, preventing the plants' roots from growing. So we used a coal rake and turned the soil over. And, after about three weeks, we started from the opposite side, making the entire field soft. We used to do this twice and our faces became wet and sticky with mud.... And there were leeches, the kind which stick to you and suck your blood. That was the way it was, when I was young.

And, about September or so, the plants would have finished growing and they would have grain. All the water which had been vital for the rice to grow would be gone to the river, and the ground would be dry and hard. The rice would turn yellow and plump by the end of October. It was beautiful to see them, waving and rustling in the wind *sara-sara, sara-sara* [rustling sound]....

The rice harvest began when the ground became dry and hard. We used sickles...using both hands, putting the plants we cut aside. Two or three days later, we tied them together with ropes or straw. Then I carried the rice stalks on my shoulder to this place where there was something like a table with holes; and women were working around it, pounding the grain off the stalks. After they had pounded it, my father used to toss the stalks over to the side.

About the time we had pounded about ten sacks of rice off the stalks, the sun was usually setting. It used to get windy at this time, and, taking advantage of this wind, my father and us, my sisters, worked together: my father threshed the rice, shaking the rice stalks, and the wind blew the hulls away; and we sisters measured the rice and put it into sacks, tying each with a rope. We put those sacks...on the cart and went home.

Tsuru Yamauchi emigrated to Hawaii in 1910. Born in 1890, she was from Itoman on the island of Okinawa, which became a prefecture of Japan in 1879. The family had once been samurai but fell on hard times and then made a living sewing clothes.

At that time, I worked with my parents, helping out when things were busy. People came from all over to have *nihongi* [kimonos] made. In winter when New Year's came, it was *awase* [lined kimonos] and *haori* [coats], and when summer came it was *hitori-mon* [unlined clothing]. They worked into the night using lamps and sewing by hand; no electricity, no sewing machines.

We lived in a small rented house of one room—about six *tatami* (padded straw mats). We used *futon* [mattresses], and the children slept, their heads all in a row.

There were seven or eight people altogether since some of the small children died soon after they were born. With them it would have been twelve children. In Itoman they'd say, "You made it, you made one dozen children!" They'd say people with children are lucky; even if you're poor, you're happy....

When I was about 13 or 14 I also learned *tofu* making, grinding the [soy] beans early in the morning. We ground it by hand and made the *tofu*. Every day it was one kettleful. In the morning, when we closed up to sell *tofu*, I got things ready for the next day. I sold *tofu* on the streets in a place like a sidewalk where things were for sale.

In 1890 the Meiji government issued the Imperial Rescript on Education, supposedly written by the emperor himself. Schoolchildren had to memorize it. The document sums up many of the ideals that the Issei brought with them to the United States:

Our Imperial Ancestors have founded Our Empire on a basis broad and everlasting and have deeply and firmly implanted virtue. Our Subjects ever united in loyalty and filial piety have from generation to generation illustrated the beauty thereof. This is the glory of the fundamental character of Our Empire, and herein also lies the source of Our education.

Ye, Our subjects, be filial to your parents, affectionate to your brothers and sisters, as husbands and wives be harmonious; as friends true; bear yourselves in modesty and moderation; extend benevolence to all; pursue learning and cultivate arts; and thereby develop intellectual faculties and perfect moral powers; furthermore always advance public good and promote common interest; always respect the Constitution and observe the laws; should emergency arise, offer yourselves courageously to the State; and thus guard and maintain the prosperity of Our Imperial Throne coeval with [which is as old as] heaven and earth. So shall ye not only be good and faithful subjects, but render illustrious the best tradition of our forefathers.

The Iwata family on the island of Hokkaido around 1914. Shigezo Iwata, in a school uniform in the back row, took this photo to the United States when he emigrated. Hokkaido is the northernmost and least populated of Japan's four main islands.

After Junji Fuyuume emigrated to the United States in the 1920s, his family sent him this photograph, taken in front of their home in Hiroshima.

Buddhist priests at a monastery in Japan around 1920. Many Japanese practice both Shinto, the ancient belief in nature spirits, and Buddhism, which was introduced to Japan in the year 552, as a "gift" from the king of Korea.

Riyo Orite was born in Hiroshima prefecture in 1885, the daughter of a farmer. As an old woman, she told an interviewer for the Issei Oral History Project about the methods used by her teacher in Japan.

When I was still a child in the countryside, a lady who was accomplished at sewing, flower arrangement, music, and many other things came to our village from Kure. She wanted to teach those things. As she couldn't find any other place, we invited her to stay with us. My strict grandmother believed that girls should be accomplished in such things, and she made me learn sewing, flower arrangement, *samisen* [a three-stringed Japanese musical instrument], and other things at home.

In those days, no music scores were available. I had to learn to play by ear. Being an old-fashioned lady, the teacher was very strict. I sat down before her, but I couldn't remember what I had learned in the previous lesson. Then she would hit me with the instrument pick. After having been hit, I was so frightened that I became worse. I cried, but I tried to learn, though I hated it. The teacher, because she was staying with us, saw whatever I was doing. I used to blow the fire with a blowpipe to cook rice. The teacher would come to me and say, "If you really want to learn *samisen*, you should hold the blowpipe as if it were a *samisen* and practice." When I cleaned our guest room, I wore a kimono with white sleeves. She would order me to hold the sleeve as a *samisen* and practice. I was scolded by her no matter where I was. Finally I quit instrument lessons because I really didn't like it.

At the age of ten I switched to sewing and flower arrangement. As the youngest one in the class, I was like a trainee. The first person who finished a flower arrangement put her work in an alcove. I had to observe it respectfully. Whenever you observe another person's flower arrangement, you are supposed to bow. Instead I stood by the flowers and touched them. The others, who were observing me from behind, laughed at my clumsiness, and I felt embarrassed.

Michiko Sato Tanaka was born in 1904 in Hiroshima. Years later, in the United States, she described for her daughter the different events of the year during her childhood.

Summers I would go with my girlfriends to swim in the river and catch locusts. We often went to Tenji mountain to collect bracken, but the climb was the joy of it: We first crossed a bridge that was only one board wide, then passed a crematory where they burned the dead bodies and stopped to look at the coffins that were black from human oils.

During the autumn there was Tanabata *matsuri* [festival]. That night the men and women *kamisama* [Shinto gods] met. We would light candles and offer melons, eggplants, and make *somen* (Japanese vermicelli). Tenjin-san *matsuri* was the festival for the scholars' gods.... ah, there were countless festivals for the myriad of Shinto shrines.

But the most happy time of the year was New Year. My parents' store was the busiest then too. There were many games to enjoy, food to feast on, and plays and movies to see. All year round there were festivals...my! how long I've been living. August 8 was the *O-bon* festival [the Feast of Lanterns]. We bought lanterns and offered them at the grave site of our dead ancestors. After *O-bon* our family would take a three-day vacation to Itsukaichi or Hatsukaichi [seaside resorts], stopping at an inn along the seaside. Tired from swimming all day, we would rest on the cool bamboo mats and gaze out from the sliding doors of our room onto the calm sea while the maids busily prepared the evening's feast. When night crept in the insects began their symphony: The grasshopper would set a steady beat—"gi-chin, gi-chin, gi-chin," and the cricket would start "koro-koro-koro," and the *suzumushi* [translated as the "bell-ring insect"] would chime in with "chin-chiri-chin-chiri-chin-chiri."

Hanayo Inouye was born in Hiroshima prefecture in 1902, the second daughter of a farming family. She came to the United States with her husband when she was 21. She told the Issei Oral History project about her girlhood.

When I was still very small, my favorite pastime was to go into the woods of nearby mountains and collect *matsutake* mushrooms. I used to take my younger brother along with me and join my friends—usually six or seven of them altogether—from the neighborhood. Along a narrow path in the mountains there were a lot of *matsutake* mushrooms hidden under fallen leaves, twigs, and other things. My brother and I didn't tell anybody about it and kept the place as our secret spot. I would go out in the streets of nearby villages and say, *"Matsutake! Matsutake!"* and some people would buy them. They were really fresh and smelled very good. The money I made on mushrooms went straight into my savings.

Japanese women in traditional dress in the 1930s. The torii gate, at right, marks the entrance to a Shinto shrine. Literally a "bird perch," the torii comes from a myth about Amaterasu, the sun goddess, who was lured from a cave by the crowing of a rooster perched outside. Many important Shinto shrines are dedicated to Amaterasu.

Shigezo Iwata, seated, with friends before he set out for the United States in 1924. In the 1920s, many young Japanese men and women adopted Western customs and dress. They were known as mobas *and* mogas—*modern boys and modern girls.*

THE DECISION TO LEAVE

Kengo Tajima was born in 1884 in Gumma prefecture, the son of a poor farmer. He emigrated to the United States to pursue theological studies and became a Christian minister. At the age of 91, he told the Issei Oral History Project:

If you would like me to tell you what motivated most Japanese men to emigrate, there are two, maybe three, reasons.... Most immigrants came from the class of small landowners. How they came to own their land I don't know. In feudal Japan all the land belonged to the Daimyo and the people tilled the land, but they really didn't own it. After the Meiji Era came a class of small landowners.

They were sort of middle-class people. Now many of our immigrants came from this class. The economic situation at the time was not stable...and many small landowners had difficulty. Families were in danger of losing their land. In order to salvage the family situation, young men emigrated. They were mostly *chonan*, eldest sons in the family. They had that responsibility; so they emigrated. They came with the idea of staying in America for three years, saving money, and then returning to restore their family fortune. Still others came because they were the second and third sons in the family, and most of the family fortune would go to the eldest son. They could shift for themselves; so they came too. That's one class.

Then came another class of more educated young men to which I belonged. One group came over after they had finished *chu gakko* (grammar school) or maybe some *gakko* (school) above. They wanted to make more of their lives; so they came over. Some schools [in Japan] did not have the privilege of military service deferment [for their students]. In order to avoid being drafted, some students came over to this country. Another reason for emigrating is that there would not be much chance for them if they stayed in Japan, because the future of most educated young men would be in government service. Tokyo University was especially built to produce government officials. Unless you went to the University of Tokyo and entered the law department and so forth, you did not have many opportunities. Those are some of the reasons why my contemporaries came over to this country.

The majority of the earliest Japanese immigrants intended to make money overseas and return to Japan. Sadama Inouye was born in 1888 in Takata prefecture, the oldest son in a family of farmers and stonecutters. He came to the United States in 1906.

After the Russo-Japanese War, Japan was poor, and the government encouraged people to go abroad to make money. By going abroad I mean Hawaii. Those who could come to the mainland were either those who were invited to come or those who were specialists in certain fields and came here to do research.

The reason I came to this country was to make money. I had one brother and two sisters. I am the second child, but the oldest son. My family farmed and we had a stone-cutting business too. My father was in debt, so he sent me to this country to make money. I sacrificed myself for my father for the first ten years in the States. I paid back all his debts. At that time I took it for granted that a child would sacrifice himself for his family, although such a situation is almost inconceivable today.

Riichi Satow, born on a farm in Chiba prefecture, came to the United States in 1912.

In those days two or three thousand dollars meant quite a lot to a Japanese person, and anybody coming back to Japan with that much money could do whatever he wanted to do—say, build a new house or buy some farm land. This was the dream that most Japanese emigrants had. Three years of hard work could bring a fortune for use back in Japan. I also had an increasing desire to come to the States, for I decided it wouldn't do any good to stay in the village. The only chance for me was to get out of there and go overseas. Japa-

"If I married well in Japan, there would be a mother-in-law, and for the kind of willful girl I am, that would be pretty hard. So my father thought I should go where there would be no in-laws...there wouldn't be much to start with, but by my own strength, I could make a go of it."

—*An Issei woman*

The Kiyonaga family of Hiroshima sent this portrait to their 18-year-old daughter Isayo in California. She had left home in 1918 to join her husband, Eiichi Yoshida.

Manjiro Nakahama

The first Japanese to live in the United States was Manjiro Nakahama, a 14-year-old fisherman. In 1841, he and four companions were swept off course in a storm and marooned on a Pacific island. A U.S. ship rescued them, and Manjiro's companions were put ashore in Hawaii. The captain of the ship, William H. Whitfield, took Manjiro to his home in New Bedford, Massachusetts.

After learning English, Manjiro attended a local school. For a while he served as a crewman on a New England whaling ship, but in 1852 homesickness caused him to return to Japan. There, Manjiro's story of his adventures saved him from execution—the usual penalty for leaving the country.

Manjiro wrote of Americans: "They tend to be a fair-skinned race, with a slightly yellow tinge to their eyes. They don't have a hereditary ruler, but elect their own 'king' according to his knowledge and ability. After four years he is succeeded by another. When the rule of a king is good...he may sit on the throne for eight years. There are some officials, but it is hard to tell them from ordinary civilians, since they don't flaunt their authority." He also noted: "American men, even officials, do not carry swords as the *samurai* do. But when they go on a journey, even common men usually carry with them two or three pistols; their pistol is somewhat equivalent to the sword of the samurai. American women have quaint customs; for instance, some of them make a hole through the lobes of their ears and run a gold or silver ring through this hole as an ornament."

In 1860, when the Japanese government sent its first diplomatic mission to the United States, Manjiro went along as an interpreter. When he returned to Japan, Manjiro took a camera and two English dictionaries. He taught the first classes in English at what is today Tokyo University. His knowledge of oceangoing ships also helped the Japanese to construct their first naval vessels.

Manjiro briefly visited the United States again in 1880, stopping at New Bedford to meet his old friend Captain Whitfield. Rewarded for his services to Japan, Manjiro lived in retirement until his death in 1898.

nese custom was such that the first son would succeed as the family head; consequently, the alternative left for the second son and down were to marry into someone's family or go someplace else to seek their own fortune—most likely to Tokyo or Osaka or to one of the other big cities. America was the first choice of places to go for almost everybody in Japan at that time. We thought lots of jobs were available and the wages were double because a dollar was worth twice as much as a yen. Our minds were filled with such dreams.

Raku Morimoto's parents emigrated from Japan to Hawaii in 1885. Morimoto later described how her parents came to the decision to leave for Hawaii.

My father was a copper-and-brass smith in Yokohama. And he was quite a drinker. [But] he was a good worker and his boss let him make a six-feet high flower vase and ten-feet high garden lamp to send to Paris for exhibition. He told me he worked right along with [the] best Japanese artist. [This artist] painted pictures, and then they have to bake them. They call them *shichihoyaki* [cloisonné]. And they [the items] were sent to Paris. [Father's boss] was very much pleased and gave him a big bonus.

Sometimes when he [father] has money, he [goes] to buy material, you see. Then his drinking friends [see] him going with the money. They call him in and instead of going to buy material, he goes with the drinking friends to the drinking place. So it seems to me my mother had a hard time.

Around that time people start to talk about Hawaii. The one thing [that] impressed her was this: Hawaii is a very good place, and there's not a dribble or drop of liquor. So my mother said, "Let's go to Hawaii."

My father said, "When you go to Hawaii I understand you have to work in the cane field. That's farm work, and I'm not suited for farm work."

But my mother said, "No, let's go; let's try and go." She spent quite a time persuading him to come.

Many young Japanese came to the United States with dreams of getting an education. In 1905, one Japanese immigrant in New York described such dreams to an interviewer.

The desire to see America was burning at my boyish heart. The land of freedom and civilization of which I heard so much from missionaries and the wonderful story of America I heard of those of my race who returned from here made my longing ungovernable. Meantime I [had] been reading a popular novel among the boys, "The Adventurous Life of Tsurukichi Tanaka, Japanese Robinson Crusoe." How he acquired new knowledge from America and how he is honored and favored by the capitalists in Japan. How willingly he has endured the hardships in order to achieve the success. The story made a strong impression on my mind. Finally I made up my mind to come to this country to receive an American education.

In the 1960s, Frank M. Tomori, who was born in Okayama prefecture in 1906, described how a movie made him decide to immigrate to America.

I happened to see a Western movie, called *Rodeo*, at the Golden Horse Theater in Okayama City, and was completely obsessed with "American fever" as a result of watching cowboys dealing with tens of thousands of horses in the vast Western plains. Enormous continent! Rich land! One could see a thousand miles at a glance! Respect for freedom and equality! That must be my permanent home, I decided.

In Japan in the early years of the 20th century, Michiko Sato Tanaka married a man who had earlier lived in the United States. Late in her life, she described for her daughter how she persuaded him to return and take her with him.

I kept coaxing Papa [her husband]. "Let's go to America." I was on the adventurous side. I wasn't afraid of anything. I wanted to see foreign countries and besides I had consented to marriage with Papa because I had the dream of seeing America. I didn't care for him much...he didn't have much education. I could have married a real good person in Japan, but I wanted to see America and Papa was a way to get there.

Grandfather Tanaka [her husband's father] said to us, "You have this much—mountains, means—America is not such a good place and besides, you may never be able to get back, so don't go." My mother wasn't happy that we were leaving, either. She said, if we stayed, she would give us the noodle shop that she had purchased and we could run it together.

But I kept urging Papa, "Let's go to America." I just couldn't wait to see it. We decided to go for a short while, make enough money for our trip, then return home. With that thought in mind, we borrowed $350 from Grandfather Tanaka and $150 from my parents and we left from Yokohama on the *Korea Maru*, bound for America. It was January 15, 1923.

Some Japanese men returned home from overseas to find wives. Natsu Okuyama Ozawa emigrated to the United States from Japan in 1924. As a woman in her 70s, she told June Namais about her wedding.

My name is Natsu, means summer. Ozawa and I came here in 1924. My husband was working here and he starts a business, export-import company: food, dry goods, all kinds of things. Then he come back to Japan to look around, wants to get married [to] someone. We got married in Japan in the Japanese way. First met my parents, they think he is good for me. Then I saw him. Then got married, that's OK. Wedding day was November 12, I think, 1923. I just reached twenty. Next year I came.

Kyutaro Abiko moved to San Francisco from Niigata prefecture in 1885. He became an important newspaperman and the founder of the Yamato Colony in California. According to Abiko:

The students who left for America from around 1882 did so because they heard that the growing economy there made it possible to work and study at the same time. Hearing this news, young men whose ambitions were stifled in Japan crossed over to America. I was one of them.

In the 19th century, the Japanese government sent young men to the United States to study so that Japan could benefit from their Western training. This group attended Rutgers College in New Jersey in 1870. Many Rutgers alumni returned home to take important posts in the Japanese government.

A Japanese family at the immigration depot in Honolulu, Hawaii, in 1885. The woman holds a samisen, a three-stringed Japanese musical instrument.

CHAPTER TWO

GOING TO AMERICA

*With tears in my eyes
I turn back to my homeland,
Taking one last look.*

This was a haiku, a poem of 17 syllables, written by one Japanese immigrant to express his feelings on leaving Japan. Bidding farewell to family and friends, and to the village where their ancestors were buried, was a wrenching experience. Carrying wicker baskets of rice, noodles, dried fish, and other food for the journey, they set out for a land they could hardly imagine.

It was relatively easy for Japanese to obtain an emigration permit. They simply had to apply to an official of their prefecture, providing a copy of their family register, which listed, for example, the place of residence and how many people lived in the household. The Japanese government tried to screen out those whose character and conduct might bring disgrace on Japan overseas.

From their homes, the emigrants made their way to one of the three major exit ports, Yokohama, Kobe, or Nagasaki. All were relatively easy to reach from any part of Japan except the sparsely populated northern regions. The Japanese government maintained a network of roads linking its major cities. The construction of railroads in the late 19th century made inland travel even easier.

The earliest Japanese emigrants often were bound for Hawaii. La-bor recruiters from Hawaii's sugar plantations distributed leaflets that described Hawaii as a paradise. The recruiters visited Japanese agricultural areas and arranged all the details of transportation. Sometimes whole families made the trip together. The recruiters guaranteed free lodging and a food allowance for all family members.

After 1891, Japanese-owned emigration companies were formed to sign laborers to contracts and arrange overseas work for them, both in the United States and Hawaii. However, these companies sometimes made false promises about wages and living conditions, and in 1894 the Japanese government issued regulations to protect the emigrants. These rules set the hours of work, amount of wages, provisions for return passage, and a requirement that "the employer shall not treat the employee cruelly or unjustly." But they also required that the employee "shall not harm his employer by carrying out shameful acts injurious of the good name of Japan...[shall] strive for friendship with his fellow workers...[shall] never behave selfishly...[and] shall be thrifty."

In the 1890s, emigrants who wished to go to the United States mainland often used the services of a Japanese emigration company. Nine of these companies were operating in Hiroshima in 1899. Though a U.S. law forbade immigrants from signing a labor contract before they arrived, Japa-nese emigration companies could arrange jobs for them after they landed. Before 1908, the majority of the Japanese emigrants to the mainland United States were male; between that year and 1924, when Asian immigration was halted by changes in U.S. laws, most new arrivals from Japan were female.

The Japanese government screened emigrants at quarantine, or isolation, stations in the ports. Before receiving a passport, would-be emigrants were tested for syphilis, hookworm, and trachoma, a common eye disease. Those headed for the United States were often examined by an American doctor as well. The Japanese examination was rigorous. In 1905 in Kobe, for example, about 60 percent failed to pass and were sent home.

The trip to Hawaii by ship took about 10 days; to the mainland, between 15 and 28 days. Most immigrants bought third-class tickets, which provided little more than a "silkworm" bunk (like a cocoon) in a room crowded with other passengers. Men and women, even married couples, were separated. Sometimes, rice and other Japanese food was served, but often not. Warned in advance about unfamiliar American food, most immigrants brought enough of their own to last the journey. One immigrant recalled, "We felt not like passengers who had paid for the trip but like criminals on a prison ship."

The passport photograph of Kokichi Masumoto, who immigrated to the United States in 1921.

Local government offices in Japan distributed instructions like this to emigrants to help them adjust to foreign customs and life. For example, emigrants were advised to carry "show money" to prove to immigration officials that they could pay their return fare if they could not find jobs.

PREPARING TO DEPART

In 1923, at the age of 21, Hanayo Inouye left her home in Hiroshima prefecture, bound for California with her husband. Years later she recalled her mother's farewell at the railway station.

When I was leaving the station, she said, "I am going to miss you very much when you leave, but I'll always be with you. We won't be separated even for a moment." At first I did not know what she was talking about. Later that night when I was undressing myself to go to sleep, I understood what she meant. I found a piece of the Buddhist altar ornament [from their home] in the breast of my kimono. I was so sad when I left her at the station that I didn't know it was there. When I found it, I thought, "She is with me after all, my mother."

Inota Tawa left Okayama prefecture in 1893, settling in Portland, Oregon. In the 1960s he remembered his departure.

My traveling possessions were one wicker trunk into which I put one blanket, two collarless flannel shirts and one small towel. No soap. No toothpaste. Usually I brushed my teeth with my finger, using salt, so I had no need of a brush.

I bought a Western suit at the Western Accessories Shop, then the only Western clothing store in Okayama City. As to my hat, it was a derby which in Japan was called a *kan-kan-bo*. I, who had suddenly become a gentleman as far as style was concerned, found myself...in high spirits.

Riyo Orite came to the United States in 1914 with her husband. Friends and relatives of the couple gave them advice.

Our neighbors brought lunches with them and came to see us off. We went to an inn with the food and had a farewell party there. Then my husband and I got on a train. My father saw me off at the train station. My mother, who was still young then, had given birth to my younger brother right before I left and couldn't come....

My husband's eldest brother saw us off too. He said, "Don't stay in the States too long. Come back in five years and farm with us." My father said, "Are you kidding? They can't learn anything in five years. They'll even have a baby over there, for five years won't be enough time to do anything. Be patient for twenty years." Hearing those words, I was so shocked that I couldn't control my tears. My father told me to return to Japan if I wasn't able to adjust to things.

Leaving home and family was a wrenching experience for the Japanese, as it was for other emigrants from other nations. Often a son who contemplated leaving consulted his father for advice on this step. One young man, who came to the United States at the end of the 19th century, received the following counsel from his father.

Above all, take it close to thy heart to live worthy of thy country. Remember that thou wilt be thrown amongst strangers of different ideas and customs. With a standard different from that to which thou hast been accustomed, and with a harsher measure, will they meet thee. Every word thou utterest falls not upon indifferent ears; every act of thy hand somebody watches. Should any action of thine dim in the least the lustre of thy country's glory or stain the brightness of thy family's records, then father me no longer father, I will no more son thee my son.

Choki Oshiro was born in 1891 in Okinawa and went to Hawaii in 1906. In an account of his life, he described his mother's reaction to his departure.

My mother...helped me get permission to go to Hawaii. She took me to the Emigration Agency; it was during the *Bon* festival in the 39th year of Meiji [1906]. The people of Naha, seeing me busy preparing for the trip, talked about me a lot. They said things like: "That woman sends such a young boy to Hawaii, you know." Although I was 15 years old and considered myself a mature man, I was still regarded as my mother's helpless child....

When I departed Naha Harbor my mother sang loudly and danced with other women relatives until the ship went out of sight. Her song went like this:..."my beloved child, on this auspicious ship, may your journey be as safe and straight as if linked by a silk thread." I cried grateful tears when friends told me about this later.

Kihachi Hirakawa was born in Matsudo, about 10 miles from Tokyo. After his father's business failed, Kihachi went to live in Yokohama, the major emigration port of Japan. In his autobiography, Hirakawa described his leaving.

The chance to go to a foreign country came when both steamship companies...lowered the fares from 50 yen to 40 yen and 35 yen to 30 yen and at last...to 25 yen only.

The English steamer, *Abyssinia*...was scheduled to sail at 10 A.M., July 27th, 1890. It was just three days before its departure, when I noticed this surprising news so I hastened quickly to the office of the Steamship Company, stated my desire to sail on the *Abyssinia*, but also added that I had no passport, and I could not obtain one in a few days. The officer said that a passport was not necessary, and if I paid my fare I would be accepted.

I did not feel satisfied, but since the company was willing to give me passage for 25 yen, I accepted their offer.

As Others Saw Them

The U.S. Commissioner of Immigration, W. M. Rice, traveled to Japan in 1899 to collect information on how that country handled its emigrants. In the report he filed, he noted that getting a passport was no easy matter:

The [Japanese] government has acted upon the theory that the character of the Japanese abroad will be taken as an index of the character of the nation at home. Hence these [emigration] regulations provide for the careful inquiry in the character of those going abroad and also require that provision shall be made for the return of the emigrant, in the event that he becomes sick or a public charge in a foreign country, before the passports are granted.

In Odawara, Japan, the Okamoto family holds a farewell party for one of its members who was leaving for the United States in 1918.

The next necessity was to secure the cash, so I borrowed 40 yen from a business man, bought a secondhand suit, a few necessary things, paid for my fare, and the balance on hand was just 10 yen, which I changed in American money, so then I had the whole sum of $8.30.

Shoshichi and Chika Saka emigrated to Hawaii in 1885 as government contract immigrants. Neither of them had been laborers in Japan. Their daughter Raku Saka Morimoto described how her mother ensured they would get a passport.

You know, farmer women always work so hard with the hands, so [their] hands are not so nice. [So my mother] said, "Oh, I have to make my hand kind of dirty-looking." She went to a vegetable store and bought *gobo* [a plant whose root is used in Japanese cooking], and touched the *gobo* many times [to] make her hands look dirty. Then she went to city hall to apply for a passport. My mother is a small woman and kind of not-so-healthy looking, you know. So, the officer over there looked at her quite a while and said, "Can you do farm work?"

My mother stretched her hand this way and she said, "*Oyakuninsama, mite kudasai. Watashi no te.*" That means "Officer, look at my hands." The officer looked at her, and finally, he issued her the passport to come to Hawaii.

In the exit ports of Kobe and Yokohama, people stayed at "emigrant houses" while waiting for their ships to depart. Sometimes the owners of these houses used tricks to keep their lodgers as long as possible, as Harry S. Kawabe recalled.

I heard that Yokohama was an easier boarding place than Kobe, so I went to Yokohama and...lodged at an emigrant house. A worker at this emigrant house took me frequently for trachoma and hookworm examinations [required for departure], but as for the most important thing—he wouldn't let me board. Presumably they were calculating to prolong my stay at the lodging house day by day. I was kept there for three weeks. I spent all my travel money there, and so I went back home, managed to get the necessary money once more, came back to Yokohama and again stayed at an emigrant house.

Finally I went aboard the English boat *Salisbury*. Western clothes were important...so I traveled in clothes given to me by my father's 35-year-old cousin—a suit, a hat, and a watch.... When I went aboard, my cousins gave me canned and bottled food.

During World War I, Tokusuke Oshiro left Okinawa with his mother to join his father in Hawaii.

My mother took care of preparations for the trip to Hawaii. She had no education and often I would interpret for her. I had to apply for a passport in Okinawa. There was something like what is now a travel agency and there were companies that would take care of the preparations for the travelers. I remember the name of the company that made our arrangements as Kakazu. They, however, made no arrangements for my job. It was just that my father called, so I was going along and didn't know what job I'd be doing.

There was no academic exam back then. The physical examination included an eye exam and an exam for hookworms.... For the eye exam, you just went to the hospital and had some medicine put in. The exam for hookworms was the hardest since you had to drink an oily medicine. I don't know what kind of medicine that was, but it was wrapped in edible rice-flour paper. You put it in a cup and drink it down whole! Some children didn't want to take it and cried. I was already 14 and knew I had to get to Hawaii in any way possible, so I said, "Yes, yes," and took it. It made my stomach run.

Osame Nagata Manago was born in Fukuoka, Japan, in 1891. She went to Hawaii in 1913. She described her inspection at Nagasaki, where her parents had come to see her off.

I was thinking about nothing but coming to Hawaii; I didn't think about anything else. At the physical inspection in Nagasaki, my eyes were fine, but I had hookworms. So I was suspended in Nagasaki for a week. My mother went home, leaving my father with me, saying she would be back when I got rid of the hookworms. She came back a few days later....

A person who'd come back from America, who helped arrange my going to Hawaii, told me to eat a lot of nuts which apparently made it difficult for the microscope to find the worms. So I ate quite a lot of these nuts which my mother roasted for me. And I must have been lucky; I was told there weren't any hookworms, so I passed. My mother and father filled up a *shingenbukuro*, cloth pouch, with persimmons, pears, candies, and rice crackers, and so many other goodies. They said I would be on board for one week to ten days, would be lonely, and should eat all of the fruits and treats.

Japanese leaving home submit their luggage for inspection at an emigrant departure point. The Japanese government also employed U.S. doctors to screen immigrants for diseases that would bar them from entering the United States.

THE VOYAGE

In 1867, Takahashi Korekiyo made the trip to America in the steerage section of the ship Colorado. *Later he returned to Japan and became a government minister. He recalled the unpleasant voyage in his autobiography.*

There was a conspicuous difference when one compared the treatment of and services for cabin [first-class] passengers and those for steerage passengers. The steerage was dark and filled with a foul odor. A large number of us were crowded into it, and each slept in one of the hammocks tied to four poles in three tiers.... About at 8 each morning, we were all cleaned and fumigated by smoking peppers for sanitary reasons. We had to eat our meals out of a large tin can together with Chinese laborers. And steerage passengers were provided with three or four large barrels which were placed on the deck where the paddlewheel was, for their need to ease nature. Straddling over two wooden boards on top of these barrels, one had to obey the calls of nature. When I went out there on the first day of the voyage, the barrels were surrounded by many Chinese, both men and women, waiting for their turn.... Since then, I dared not go near that place. Instead, I managed to sneak into the toilet for cabin passengers whenever they had all gone to the dining salon.

Chojiro Kubo, born in 1880 in Yamaguchi prefecture, left for the United States when he was 17. He recalled conditions aboard his ship, the Yamaguchi Maru.

The third class accommodations were crowded with more than 160 passengers and there wasn't any bunk in which to rest. I slept spreading my own mat and blanket on the wooden floor in the front hatch where there were no windows and no lights. Overhead a piece of net was hung, and when the boat rolled we clung to the net to keep from being thrown around. Day after day the weather was bad and the sea stormy. The hatch was tightly closed and there was no circulation of air, so we were all tortured by the bad odor. As the boat was small, whenever a high wave hit us the top deck was submerged and the sound of the screw [propeller] grinding in empty space chilled us. The food was second class Nankin rice and salted kelp, with dirty clams preserved by boiling in soy sauce. It was impossible fare which now I wouldn't dare to eat. I shivered, thinking that I would proably go back to Japan some years later in just such a boat. Everyone was groggy with seasickness.

The ship City of Tokio *took the first Japanese contract laborers to Hawaii in 1885. About 1,000 men, women, and children made the voyage.*

Saburo Hirata, who left from the port of Yokohama in 1908 when he was 22, had lively memories of his trip.

During the 16 days from Yokohama to Seattle, talent shows were held on board. People applauded the *noh* [Japanese theater] singing, popular songs, *shigin* [chanting of Chinese poems], and *biwa* [Japanese guitar] solos, as well as Japanese dramas. The boat boiled with youthful activity. A certain gentleman from Hiroshima prefecture who had apparently studied in advance, explained the American situation in detail to us all, saying that he had no difficulty with English conversation. One day we saw him talking to a white lady who was taking a walk on the top deck. He was frantically using gestures, while the lady grimaced and finally reproved [scolded] him by saying, in perfect Japanese, "You aren't making any sense. Study English more!" Mr. "Certain Gentleman" blushed, and we all burst into laughter.

Many years after Chiyokichi Kyono emigrated from Kobe to join her parents in the United States, she recalled her unpleasant introduction to American food on board ship.

At the time, I was only a freshman in middle school, had just learned the alphabet, and had no confidence whatever in my English. Of course I knew absolutely nothing about the American way of life. According to Japanese custom, we chose a menu of bean soup (*miso*) and pickles for breakfast, but one morning we decided, "Why not try a Western meal?" and we switched from the Japanese to the Western menu. Square slices of bread were served with a yellow lump. I thought it must be some kind of radish pickle, and carelessly I put the yellow lump into my mouth.

Ugh! I still remember that I spontaneously uttered a sound similar to a scream. It was butter, not one bit like a radish pickle! To tell the truth I had never before met up with such a material as "butter." It melted in my mouth, felt sticky, and I couldn't stand the smell.

Hanayo Inouye recalled the smells and sights of her 1923 voyage to the United States, which she made with her husband.

We came on the *Tenyo Maru*. On the way to Yokohama from Kobe the sea was very rough. I became so awfully seasick that I truly thought I was going to die. It was my first experience on such a big ship. Although I was all right after Yokohama, a lot of people suffered from severe cases of seasickness all the way. They threw up whatever they had eaten, and because of that they were having a hard time even standing up on their own. I can't forget how much I hated to go to the bathroom, for it was way upstairs. Everytime I had to climb up these steep stairs, I tried desperately not to fall off. Oh, it was really scary. Another thing that bothered everyone on board was the smell of paint. It was terrible on top of the seasickness.

The Tamura family of Oregon kept this photograph of Issei immigrants leaving Japan for the United States in 1907. The following year, in the Gentlemen's Agreement, Japan agreed to stop permitting laborers to emigrate to the United States.

I was on the ship for over two weeks.... I missed my mother, and I was so lonely that I cried every night.

—Mrs. Ko Takakoshi, who came to the United States in 1918

Japanese immigrants on board a ship headed for the United States in the 1920s. Until 1924, the wives and children of immigrants who had arrived earlier were allowed to enter the United States.

Our beds were on racks. Men slept in one section, and women slept in another. We could spend the day together, but we were separated through the night. Well, one time a woman asked for a comb, so I let her use mine. Then, when I combed my hair with it later, my head became really itchy all over. There weren't good facilities to wash my hair on the ship. As soon as we landed, I rushed to a drugstore, and took care of it. It was lice from her hair! The sanitary situation on the ships in those days was very poor.

All I could see from the ship was just the blue sea, day after day. I kept wondering when in the world the voyage would be over, so I was truly relieved when I saw seagulls flying over us.

Tokusuke Oshiro, who as a young boy traveled from Yokohama to Hawaii with his mother, recalled some of the pranks he played on board ship.

The name of our ship was the *Shunyo-maru.* This was during World War I and Japan was allied with the U.S. A Japanese warship would watch us, and at night we had to turn off the lights.

The women and men were in separate rooms. Being a child, I was with my mother in the women's side. The women all took care of me even though I'd do mischief. When they were sleeping, I'd take some ink and draw a moustache, and I remember being chased!...

When we were nearing Honolulu, we had a party for the safe trip. They showed moving pictures, and because I was only looking there, I didn't see a Negro boat-boy who was sleeping right where I was walking. I just stepped over him and went over there. Then I got surprised and looked back. Really, I should have apologized, but since I was a child, I became afraid and just ran away!...

On the ship, I wasn't really worried, but as we came out to the middle of the Pacific, sometimes it'd be rough and the wave would be over us. I used to wonder, "Would this reach the destination?" But we finally arrived at Honolulu.

Minejiro Shibata was born in 1902, the son of a farmer in Shizuoka prefecture. He came to the United States in 1919, when he was 17 years old. Years later, he remembered the loneliness he felt on his voyage.

I think I came on the *Saibei Maru* in 1919. After stopping in Hawaii overnight, the ship went directly to San Francisco. Almost everybody on board was an immigrant. Eating was the only thing I did on the ship. The food served on board wasn't especially good, but I didn't mind. I didn't know anybody; so I had no friends or acquaintances to talk to and stayed on deck most of the time. With tears in my eyes, I watched other ships sailing in the distance. I also remember that lice bred in the ship because we couldn't take a bath too often. I can never forget that.

Choki Oshiro had an eventful voyage across the Pacific to Hawaii on the Mongolia, *as he remembered in his autobiography.*

We were told the ship would reach Hawaii in less than 20 days. However, after one week, the ship ran aground near Midway island. All of us worked to move things from the front to the rear, hoping this would free the ship from the reef. The ship would not move and we began throwing heavy things overboard, keeping records of the things lost. A [Japanese] navy ship, the *Anegawa*, was in the area but could not rescue us because she did not have enough fuel. So, we landed on Midway and stayed in a tent for about a week....

There was nothing but the [U.S.] Army Camp on this small island; all we could see were miles and miles of water. There were many sea birds that seldom flew. When we chased them, they would escape to the ocean and swim away. It was good exercise because we slept better after chasing the birds. We got fresh water by simply digging about two feet down. And I recall the nights when small crabs came out and pinched our legs and arms. We all wished that a rescue boat would come quickly so we could get out of the mess. In the meantime, we discovered a Japanese cook in the camp and enjoyed visiting with him.

Finally, after a week, a boat named the *Siberia* came and rescued us—our dream come true. Then as the boat started to sail a strange thing happened: the *Mongolia*, which had remained stuck on the reef, started to move. She sailed with the *Siberia* all the way to Honolulu.

Well-dressed passengers, most of them Japanese, land in San Francisco around 1930. Because a 1924 U.S. immigration law effectively banned Japanese immigration, it is likely that most of these people were merchants or students. The Japanese government stamped their passports "nonemigrant." However, a small number of them actually settled permanently in the United States.

Japanese immigrants arrive at Angel Island, the landing station in San Francisco Bay. Opened in 1908, Angel Island was the major entry port for Asian immigrants after that time. However, some Japanese took ships to Seattle or Vancouver, Canada, because they had heard immigration officials were more lenient there.

PORTS OF ENTRY

A strong current in the Pacific Ocean—called *kuroshiwo*, or "black current," in Japanese—flows northeast to the Aleutian Islands and then south to the west coast of North America. Throughout history, Japanese fishing boats were caught in this current, carried off course, and thought to be lost at sea. Some modern scholars think it possible that Japanese arrived in America via the black current centuries ago.

The earliest historical record of such a voyage dates from 1833, when three Japanese fishermen staggered ashore near Cape Flattery in today's Washington State. Dr. John McLoughlin, who commanded a nearby trading post of the Hudson's Bay Company, heard that some Native Americans had taken the Japanese prisoner. He sent soldiers to rescue them, and they were eventually returned to the China coast, since Japan did not permit most European ships to dock at its ports at that time.

The first Japanese to become an American citizen was another such "bird of passage," Hamada Hikozo. Along with 16 companions, he was rescued from a drifting fishing boat in 1850, when he was just 13. Hikozo went to Baltimore, Maryland, where he

was baptized a Christian, taking the name Joseph Heco. He became an American citizen in 1858. Three years later, Heco met President Abraham Lincoln, who appointed him interpreter for the American consulate in Kanagawa, Japan.

Just how Joseph Heco was able to obtain U.S. citizenship is something of a puzzle. A 1790 U.S. law specified that "any alien, being a free white person" could become a naturalized citizen. Most Japanese immigrants who arrived after Heco were denied citizenship because they were of the "Mongolian" race, or Asian. Even when the naturalization law was amended in 1873 to permit immigrants "of African nativity or descent" to become citizens, the Supreme Court ruled that Asians were still not eligible for citizenship.

The first Japanese laborers arrived in Hawaii in 1868. Called *gannen-mono*, or "first-year people" (because they left home in the first year of the Meiji emperor's reign), they had been recruited in the streets of Tokyo, Yokohama, and other large cities. These city dwellers were not used to the hard labor of chopping sugarcane, and most soon returned home.

Large-scale immigration to Hawaii did not begin until 1885, when a ship called the *City of Tokio* arrived in Honolulu Bay

with nearly 1,000 men, women, and children. They were temporarily housed in a *senningoya* ("hut for 1,000 people") on Sand Island in the harbor. The island later became the main entry station for Japanese immigrants to Hawaii. There they were given a medical exam to test their fitness for the hard work in the fields.

Although some Japanese students and traders arrived in the mainland United States during the early years of the Meiji reign, the census of 1880 showed only 148 Japanese residents. In 1882, however, prejudice against another Asian group—the Chinese—resulted in a law that virtually banned new immigrants from China. This created an opportunity for Japanese immigrants to take the kinds of jobs formerly held by Chinese. By 1910, there were more than 72,000 Japanese residents on the mainland and nearly 80,000 in Hawaii, which by that time had become a U.S. territory. Some Japanese came first to Hawaii and then went on to the mainland; a number traveled back and forth frequently.

The students who arrived in San Francisco in the early years of immigration often found a place to stay at the Gospel Society and other institutions founded by Christian churches. There, they could get free meals and lodging as well as elementary English lessons.

Later, Japanese emigration companies hired representatives to meet the immigrants at the dock in American West Coast cities. The newcomers would be taken to a Japanese-operated inn or boardinghouse. There, they felt secure among others who spoke their language and ate familiar Japanese food. They could stay until they found jobs, which were usually obtained through the innkeepers.

Members of the first generation of Japanese immigrants, called *Issei*, faced the same kinds of racial prejudice that the Chinese immigrants had endured. In 1907, President Theodore Roosevelt began negotiations with the Japanese government that resulted in the so-called Gentlemen's Agreement of 1908. The Japanese government agreed to stop issuing passports to laborers bound for the United States. Students and merchants could still come, but they had formed only a small percentage of Japanese immigrants. In addition, President Roosevelt issued an executive order that blocked Japanese laborers in Hawaii from coming to the mainland.

The Gentlemen's Agreement was not successful in halting Japanese immigration, however. About 160,000 additional Japanese immigrants arrrived in the United States between 1908 and 1924—more than had arrived in all the previous years. (These figures do not include Hawaii.) The immigration did not stop because the Gentlemen's Agreement had an important loophole: wives or other close family members of men who were already living in the United States were allowed to immigrate. Before 1908, about seven out of eight Japanese residents on the mainland were

Japanese women cook a meal at the senningoya *("hut for 1,000 people") on Sand Island at Honolulu, Hawaii, around 1885. Sand Island became the main entry station for Japanese immigrants to Hawaii.*

men. The ensuing years saw a sharp increase in the number of women, producing a ratio of about four women to six men by 1924.

Many of the women immigrants of this time were "picture brides." A man seeking a wife would have his picture taken in the United States. Usually he tried to appear as prosperous as possible, sometimes by borrowing a suit and tie, even though his everyday clothes might be those of a farm laborer. He sent the photograph to his family, who showed it to families of similar background with marriageable daughters. When one of them

showed interest, her photograph was mailed to the prospective husband. If he agreed, the couple was married in a Buddhist ceremony in Japan—even though the husband was across the Pacific Ocean, thousands of miles away. The bride then set out to meet her husband in Hawaii or the United States.

Marriages arranged by parents were part of the traditional society of Japan. It was not very different for a woman to choose a husband in America so that she could emigrate.

On arrival in Honolulu, San Francisco, or Seattle—the major ports of entry for Japanese immigrants—the young woman searched the faces of the crowd waiting on shore. She compared them with the picture she carried in the sleeve of her kimono. Often it was difficult to recognize her husband, for some men sent pictures taken years before.

Even if the picture was accurate, it could not reveal the personality of the man. The picture brides' dreams of happiness did not always come true. As one of them, Ai Miyasaki, recalled, "Many Issei mothers suffered much, but they could not afford to go back to Japan. Their expectations were great, so the disappointment was as great."

Newcomers were also given a physical examination. One woman recalled, "The inspector said, 'Smell bad! Don't come too close!' I was upset at being treated like a dirty pig....The inspector felt our joints at both elbows, around the neck, and on both sides of the groin. Of course it was done while we were fully dressed, but I felt insulted and became furious."

In 1908, the United States opened an immigration station at Angel Island in San Francisco Bay, where new arrivals from Asia were questioned about their eligibility to enter the country. Picture brides were sometimes suspected of being prostitutes and they had to present marriage certificates before being allowed to leave the island.

Japanese magazines that gave advice to immigrants reported that American immigration officials were more lenient in Seattle, Washington, than they were in San Francisco. A Japanese consular official in Seattle wrote a letter to his government explaining why so many immigrants chose to enter the United States there. For the "tax" of one dollar (actually a bribe), immigration officials would let anyone through. According to the Japanese magazines, it was even simpler to land at the Canadian cities of Victoria or Vancouver, just across the border, and then enter the United States by ferry boat.

By 1920, there were about 111,000 Japanese in the mainland United States—about one-tenth of 1 percent of the total population.

(Another 109,000 lived in Hawaii, which was not yet a state.) Most lived on the West Coast, where

Contract laborers with their baggage at Honolulu in the late 19th century. The cost of the voyage would be deducted from their wages of $13 a month.

prejudice against them was strong. Congressmen from California and other western states urged the U.S. government to stop Japanese immigration. In 1920, the Japanese and American governments negotiated what was called the "Ladies' Agreement," in which Japan agreed to stop issuing passports to picture brides.

In 1924, the United States passed a comprehensive immigration law that barred anyone "ineligible for citizenship" from legally entering the country. In effect, this closed the door to further Japanese immigration because

Asians were at that time not allowed to become naturalized citizens. (Two years earlier, the U.S. Supreme Court had denied a Japanese immigrant's application for citizenship because he was "clearly...not Caucasian.")

The era of the Issei immigrants was over. From then until 1965, any significant increase in the Japanese American population resulted from births of second-generation Nisei and their children, the Sansei.

Except for a small number of "war brides" of American servicemen after World War II, Japanese immigrants were not allowed legal entrance to the United States until 1952. That year the U.S. Congress passed the Immigration and Nationality Act, which legally eliminated race as a bar to entry. However, the act set regional quotas that sharply limited the number of Asians allowed to enter the United States. Japan was allotted only 185 new immigrants per year.

Passage of the Immigration Act of 1965 opened the doors to America once more. This act abolished quotas based on national origin and instead allowed 170,000 legal immigrants per year from the Eastern Hemisphere, with a maximum of 20,000 per country. In addition, the spouses, children, and parents of previous immigrants were granted exemptions from the quota.

The medical examination room at Angel Island. Immigrants were checked for ailments such as syphilis, hookworm, and trachoma, a common eye disease. Because the Japanese government also required such exams at the exit ports, relatively few immigrants were turned back at Angel Island.

U.S. immigration officials at Angel Island question new arrivals about their eligibility to enter the country.

ARRIVAL

Shoshichi and Chika Saka came to Hawaii in 1885 as government contract laborers. Chika was so seasick during the voyage that she could only drink water. Her daughter Raku Saka Morimoto described her arrival at the immigration station on Sand Island.

Somehow she was alive when she landed here. Two men had to carry her into what they call *senningoya*. That means "a house full of 1,000 people," so must be great big house on Sand Island. While she was there she looked around and saw the place was so muddy, and grass houses here and there. Then [she] saw fat, dark-colored, barefooted Hawaiian women walking around the place. She said she couldn't stop crying. She thought it [would be] much better than that. (Laughs.)

But she said King Kalakaua was very kind to them. To the children, he used to send candies and fruits. He came to see the immigrants, you see. He said, "Let them form double line." He walked between them, stretching both hands and shook hands with them.

So my father used to say, "I'm very proud of two things."

I said, "What are they?"

He said, "I worked with the best artist in Japan, and then I came to Hawaii and I shook hands with King Kalakaua."

Tokushiga Kizuka was born in Fukuoka prefecture in 1901. His parents emigrated to the United States when he was six, leaving him with relatives. When he was seventeen, his father summoned him to follow.

My father came to meet me when I landed in San Franciso. Other than a picture, I had no idea how my father looked, and I did not recognize him—it was like we were strangers. At the immigration bureau, there was another passenger named Honda. His father thought I was his son, because his son was very big when he was young, and my father thought I was Honda, because I was small when I was a young boy.

When Minejiro Shibata went to San Francisco to join his father in 1919, he had to stay for a while at the immigration station on Angel Island.

I arrived in March and stayed on Angel Island for three or four days in order to go through the immigration procedures…. They treated us neither too well nor too badly at the immigration office. I didn't care about the treatment, for I didn't have to pay for anything. The only thing I didn't like

was the bathroom. There were a lot of toilet bowls side by side without any doors. I, being Japanese, couldn't stand it. They took our feces and examined it. They also examined us to see if we had a skin disease. I was released after that.

Eijiro Ogawa, who arrived in the United States from Gunma prefecture in 1917, worked his way across the Pacific on the ship Ide Maru. *A friend had advised him that after the ship docked in Tacoma, Washington, he could slip ashore without a passport.*

During the night of December 6, when the *Ide Maru* was sliding away from the pier, I left all my possessions behind and jumped overboard onto some logs which were piled on the pierside, and hid, holding my breath.

As advised by Mr. Kawaguchi, I stole through the streets of Tacoma. It began to sleet. Thinking that if I were caught, all my effort would come to nothing, I walked on and on, in fact almost ran in the sleet, with the lights of the town behind me and the distant fields ahead. In my pocket there was one ten-yen coin. As I had left everything in my wicker trunk on board and hadn't even put on an outer coat, the ice-cold sleet soon penetrated my suit. I didn't know where I was. The expression on my face must have been desperate. I finally arrived at the edge of town, after being barked at by many a dog, and there I found a wood-burning locomotive standing idle. Crawling up on the wood-pile, I fell sound asleep.

Morning! I woke up to the sound of an auto—prrt! prrt! and a white man was looking at me suspiciously. At first instantly I put up my fists, but then changed the gesture to one of prayerfulness and pleading, as if to say, "Please let me go!" With gestures he ordered me to help him unload the wood from the engine, and I did what he asked. He took me in his truck to the house of his boss. Since I couldn't speak English, I couldn't understand at all what they were saying. There I was served breakfast and paid $2 for helping to unload the wood. After saying goodbye I walked on and on, in the opposite direction from the port. I finally found a Japanese farmer's house at the place called Firwood.

PICTURE BRIDES

Picture brides at Angel Island. In 1900, there were only 410 married Japanese women in the United States. By 1920, the year that the Japanese government stopped issuing passports to picture brides, there were 22,193.

Tatsuyo Hazama was a picture bride who went to Hawaii to join her husband. Interviewed when she was in her 80s, she recalled their first meeting.

In 1919, when I was an 18-year-old living in the Hiroshima countryside, a nakahodo [marriage broker] came to ask my parents for my hand in marriage to a young man in far away Hawai'i. The nakahodo brought a picture of a young man standing in a dark American suit. I'll never forget walking very far with my mother to have my picture taken to send to Hawai'i. When we and our families had agreed on the marriage, it was recorded in the *Koseki Tohon* in Hiroshima. I had no problem in accepting the arrangement because it was the Japanese custom for parents and the nakahodo to arrange the marriages....

As we docked, I looked down and recognized my husband from the photograph; but we were not allowed to meet or talk together for about a week. We were taken straight to the immigration station for another inspection. We were all afraid of the inspector who was Japanese for he talked loudly, scolded everyone, and ordered us around. Once, he grabbed my hairdo and said: "Get rid of your *nezumi* (rat)." It was the style to wear a high hairdo with a cushion inside to give it body, so I had one of those in my hair.

When the day finally came for us to meet our husbands, we excitedly helped to dress each other in a *montsuki*, special kimono with a crest, and a fancy sash called a *maruobi*. Outside the immigration station, our husbands waited eagerly for a glimpse of us. We were nervous and shy, I thought my husband was tall and handsome. We rode in a two horse carriage to Onomichiya Hotel. The next day, my husband and his brother took us to see Waikiki [Beach].

Two days later, we went by boat to Lihue, Kaua'i, to live on the plantation. We were already married in Japan, but we did have a party. The people in the camp prepared the food for the celebration which was held in the social hall.

Tsuru Yamauchi came to Hawaii in 1910 as a picture bride. She remembered how frightened she was when she met her husband.

I couldn't talk to Yamauchi-*san* [her new husband], because I didn't know him. Even when he spoke, I couldn't answer. That's how it was, you know. And I was so stubborn then.

He had taken me from the Immigration Bureau where we all had been waiting three or four days. They had all the people who'd been sent for sit on a couch. The people who came to get us saw us on the couch. "I'm being taken away by a man today," I thought, frightened at the idea. Those who came as picture brides with me were holding me down; I was trembling so much, scared. We'd seen their pictures, so when they came, we thought, "Oh, my husband," and all the people sitting were happy. I saw Yamauchi-*san*'s picture and knew what he looked like too, but I never had much contact with boys, so I was afraid. After all, my parents had strictly warned us girls. When the sun went down, they said, "Don't go out," and they didn't let us out.

But these more experienced women who were holding on to my shaking legs were saying, "When they come to get us, we'll all be taken away, so don't be scared." Well, Yamauchi-*san* claimed me when they brought him over, and he said, "It's her." Then they let us leave together. When he took me to Waipahu where we would live in the middle of the canefield, I really felt homesick.

Hideyo Yokoyama, born in Hiroshima in 1897, had a rude shock when she arrived in the United States as a picture bride.

I landed in Seattle at the age of 22 in April, 1920. My husband was 13 years older than I. I had heard that he was a dentist, but I found out he was a truck driver. Since the truth was so different from what the go-between had said, I was disgusted. When I left Kobe via the *Africa Maru* my dream, though vague, was still a dream. When I boarded, a lady about 30 years old told me, "America is not a place where an innocent girl like you should go." I didn't understand what she meant then, but I understood soon enough upon arrival, and was disappointed.

On the day I landed we had the wedding ceremony, but I wanted to go back to Japan as soon as possible. I wrote my parents in Hiroshima. My father had told me, "If you don't like it there, then come back." But I had no money for a ticket to return. So I was caught by fate and consigned to live in America permanently.

When Kakuji Inokuchi was 97, he remembered waiting for his picture bride decades before at the Immigrant Station in Honolulu.

There were ten of us who went to pick up our ten brides. My wife and I had already been married two years by having her registered in our family records back in Japan. She was the niece of my friend who had returned to Japan earlier. I asked him to look around for a wife for me and he said he thought his niece was best. He sent me her picture, so I knew what she looked like. Oh, she was the prettiest of all the girls there; she was even prettier than her picture. My heart just pounded with joy because I was so proud of her. She didn't look disappointed when she saw me, and I was so happy about that too.

These are the pictures that 18-year-old Tami Ishahara (top) and 29-year-old Masashi Ishahara exchanged before they were married. At an immigration hearing on Angel Island in January 1910, Tami testified that she "married [him] by photograph in July 1909" while she was living with her parents in Japan. Her husband owned a laundry in Santa Barbara, California.

39

At first glance these Japanese looked like good people. They were brimming with vigor and zest. These people from the Empire of Japan did not appear to have visited foreign countries before and strolled through the streets as if they were enjoying the novelty of it all very much.

They are of a very polite race. They quickly took to our greeting, "Aloha!" and repeatedly returned the courtesy with "Aloha, Aloha."

In spite of their shabby clothing, they did not appear to be timid in the least. On the whole they created a favorable impression and were greeted warmly by white residents and natives alike. It is hoped that they will turn out to be amiable and useful workers.

FIRST IMPRESSIONS

Sakiko Suyama remembered her difficulty in adjusting to American-style clothing.

Married in 1913, I landed in Tacoma following my husband who had gone to the States just one step ahead of me. First of all we bought outfits of Western clothes at Hara's. When I landed I was in a kimono with a maroon-colored pleated over-skirt, my hair arranged in a bun.

At that time one complete outfit of Western clothes cost between $25 and $28. The corset was so tight that women couldn't bend over. I had to ask my husband to tie my shoe strings! Some girls' corsets were so tightly laced that they fainted. There were stories hard to laugh at about men carrying their brides over the doorsill and hastily trying to untie the corset strings. I, in a big hat and high laced shoes, wearing a high-necked blouse and trailing skirt belted and buckled at the waist—and of course for the first time in my life a brassiere and a bustle (hip-pad). The trouble was the underwear! Japanese women were only accustomed to use petticoats. Wearing Western panties for the first time, I frequently forgot to pull them down when I went to the toilet so I often got them wet. Though I had heard about life in America before I left Japan, once I actually landed I was amazed. If I had known more in detail beforehand, I would probably never have come.

Okumura's Boarding House on Kukui Street in Honolulu. Japanese-operated boardinghouses provided familiar food and a place where immigrants could stay until they found jobs. Boardinghouse keepers often received commissions for supplying workers to plantation recruiters.

Riyo Orite came to the United States in June 1914 with her new husband. They stayed at the Fuji Hotel in Seattle, whose owner was from a neighboring town in Hiroshima prefecture. Here she learned that she and some other female companions had made a mistake in getting dressed.

Some Japanese ladies who had returned from the States decided not to go back, and they gave their Western clothing to the other Japanese ladies who were planning to go. There was underwear made of lace, but they didn't know how to wear it. I was in a black suit dress, which wasn't as beautiful as the lace underwear. I thought the dresses made of lace looked beautiful. They should have worn the lace wear under the dress, but they'd worn it on top! We found out after we got to the hotel. Hillbillies! The hotel owner's wife was surprised and laughed at those ladies when we got there. She was amazed, "How daring you are to have traveled in such a fashion!" Then we found out the truth. I was in a dress which I had bought in Kobe. One of my husband's cousins came to Seattle to meet us and told me that I had put on a blouse with the front side in back!

Riichi Satow was born in Chiba prefecture in 1895 and emigrated to the United States at the age of 17. Later on, he recalled his first impressions.

When the ship came into the San Francisco port, I felt, "Good, I finally made it!" I didn't think about the future, but I was simply glad to have arrived. One thing that caught my attention was the shape of the houses. They were all square and looked like boxes, really different from Japanese houses! The city itself was rather beautiful, despite the earthquake [six years earlier]. Right from there I got on a train to go to the country, to Napa. Along the way I saw windmills, a lot of them. I remember wondering about those things. Then someone explained that they were to pump water.

Nisuke Mitsumori came to the United States in 1905. It was during the Russo-Japanese War, and in the United States anti-Japanese prejudice was on the rise, as Mitsumori learned upon his arrival.

It was March or April of 1905 when I landed in San Francisco. A man from a Japanese inn was at the port to meet me with a one-horse carriage. There was a gang of scoundrels who came to treat the immigrants roughly as soon as they heard that some Japanese had docked.... There were a group of fifteen to twenty youngsters who shouted, "Let's go! The Japs have come!" We rushed to the inn to avoid being hit. As we went along, we were bombarded with abuses such as "Japs," "lewd," et cetera. They even picked horse dung off the street and threw it at us. I was baptized with horse dung. This was my very first impression of America.

The Japanese American Lost Colony

The first Japanese who came to the mainland United States with the intention of settling permanently arrived in California in May 1869. This group of 22 people included samurai, farmers, tradesmen, and four women. Back in Japan, the feudal lord they had served had lost his lands because of the Meiji government's reforms, and they set out for the United States to establish a new settlement. The colonists brought tea seeds and mulberry trees (on which silkworms feed), and obtained about 600 acres of land near Placerville, California. They gave their community the name Wakamatsu Tea and Silk Farm Colony.

Unfortunately, the climate in that part of California was dryer than in Japan. The seedlings and trees withered and died, and the colony broke up less than two years later. All that remains of it today is a tombstone with the epitaph: "In memory of Okei, died 1871, age 19 years, a Japanese girl."

Little is known about what happened to the rest of the colonists, although one of them, Kuninosuke Masumizu, settled in Sacramento, opened a fish store, and married. His wife was the daughter of a Native American and a former slave.

In 1969, when a local newspaper noted the 100th anniversary of the founding of the Wakamatsu Colony, Masumizu's descendants were found to be still living in the Sacramento area. The family name was now Elebeck, and they considered themselves to be African Americans.

Michiko Sato Tanaka came to the United States in 1923, with her husband, who had already spent time in America. Michiko later told her daughter:

About two weeks from the day we left Japan, we landed in San Francisco. From that moment on, I began to understand the world. We first went to the Aki Hotel and ate *miso shiru* (bean paste soup), *iwashi* (sardines), and *daikon oroshi* (grated white radish). It was clean there. But when we came to Liberty (a town in northern California), the conditions were terrible. I thought America was supposed to be a beautiful, clean country, but it was dirtier than Japan.

We stayed at Ishikawa's boarding house. The walls were plastered with pictures from magazines, the floors were dirt, and there was only one bed. Papa said, "Well, this is it." From the window I caught a glimpse of farmers in overalls shooting guns and I thought, What an ugly place.

Liberty had a Japanese population of approximately 500 people, of whom very few were women. Everyone knew Papa there and they made a big fuss because he had come back with a wife. It was very rare for a man to have a wife.

Osame Nagata Manago went to Hawaii as a picture bride in 1913. She described her trip from Honolulu to her husband's home.

We left Honolulu [after a ceremony with a Shinto priest] for Kona [on the island of Hawaii] that day at noon. But our boat was something else. We were put together with horses and cattle. I only kept wondering how could we go on a boat like that. I remember it clearly—the cow dung and all. I asked my husband if that was how we were going. And it was. I went sitting on the boards, leaning against my *yanagi-gori* [wicker trunk]. We couldn't lie down, we had to be sitting up all the way to Kona. My husband told me that everything, people, cattle, cargo went together, and even if you asked, there was no more room. The boat arrived offshore of Kona, and a canoe, you know, a little boat, came to get us. They handed me down to the canoe with a count of "One, two, three." They did the same to my husband and to my *yanagi-gori*.

In Kailua, there was a landing, made of lumber; that's where the canoe landed. The canoe was lower than the landing, so they pulled my hands while the others pushed me up, and I came out of the canoe. That's how we came in those days. It was really pitiful. And for the cattle and horses, they tied them by the neck to the canoe and let them swim, then they would lift them up.

So we arrived at Kailua about six o'clock in the morning. There was a small restaurant. We rested there for a while. We waited for a person who was supposed to come and pick us up. Since I had been told that there would be a celebration party [for the arrival of the picture bride], I washed my face, changed into my lilac *montsuki*, crested kimono, with a pretty *obi*, and

Rihei Onishi (holding the baby) took his family from Japan to Texas in 1903. He and a group of 15 other immigrants introduced a new variety of rice that flourished in the Texan soil.

was ready to go. Then a man came down with a horse and carriage with four poles standing up. I was told to hold onto a pole since the road was rough and full of rocks. Guava tree branches hit the carriage, *Batan! Batan! Batan!* [Japanese bang]. We were told not to stick our faces out since we'd get hurt. Really it was terrible. When we got to [the town of] Captain Cook, it was twelve o'clock noon.

So we arrived at a place a little beyond ours.... Because it was a wedding celebration, everybody was waiting for us. They stood in front of the house, saying "Welcome back, Mr. Manago," to my husband, and "Welcome, you must be exhausted!" to me. When the party started, it was just like Japan. Everybody was dancing and singing, just having a jolly good time. Everybody was very kind to me from the time I arrived.

Because he was accepted as a student by the Union Theological Seminary in New York, Toru Matsumoto was able to enter the United States after the 1924 exclusion act. In the 1930s, Matsumoto landed in San Francisco. A Japanese friend had arranged for him to meet Jay and Mary, a honeymooning couple who would drive him to New York City.

They drove too fast for me, sometimes 80 or 90 miles an hour—and they kissed while driving. Since they cared so much for each other, I wondered why they didn't value their lives more.

I was amazed at the vastness of the country, there being often more than 100 miles between sizable towns. Because I saw so much land and so few people, I grew uneasy and said to Jay, "Why do you waste so much good soil here? Don't you know about the famines and overcrowding in other countries?"

"Well, we don't want to produce too much, because that spoils the price of farm products. We don't want foreigners to come and make a living here because it lowers the standard of living." Jay said it in such a way that I could tell he was joking....

My first view of New York was through the rain from the 125th Street Ferry.... One of my greatest surprises was to see the sun on the street pavements, for all the pictures of New York which I had seen showed only the tall skyscrapers, and gave the impression that the streets were sunless tunnels.

I didn't understand the conversation of people in buses and subways, and I was miserable to think my English was so poor. If I asked some stranger the way to the post office, he would shout, "That way, and turn right." In such cases, I thought the loud voice was due to anger, not realizing that people thought that foreigners could understand them better if they spoke loudly....

I got another shock and a rather frustrating surprise when I discovered that practically no one with whom I talked knew that the United States had an exclusion law, and that I could not become an American citizen because of it. In Japan we thought of the law as an expression of the will of the whole American people. Here almost no one knew about it.

The Hotel Ohio in Portland, Oregon, around 1915. The proprietors were Tomoichi Sumida and Mosaburo Matsushima. Japanese-owned boardinghouses and hotels like this one were often the first destination of newly arrived immigrants.

Settlers gather at the railroad depot in the Florida Yamato Colony, founded by Jo Sakai, a Japanese immigrant who graduated from New York University's business school in 1903. One of the colony's members, George Morikami, became wealthy by investing in land after World War II. He established a park and museum of Japanese culture in Delray Becah, Florida.

Many Japanese men found work on the western railroads in the early part of the 20th century. After the United States banned Chinese immigration in 1882, labor contractors for the railroads began to hire Japanese immigrants.

CHAPTER FOUR

GOING TO WORK

Hawaii, Hawaii
Like a dream
So I came
But my tears
Are flowing now
In the canefields

Before leaving Japan, laborers who came to the Hawaiian plantations after 1885 signed contracts that bound them to their employers, usually for three years. The contract laborers found that Hawaii was not the "paradise" that recruiters had described. They lived in communal bunkhouses with other immigrant workers, such as Chinese, Koreans, Filipinos, Portuguese, and Puerto Ricans. At five A.M. a whistle blew and *lunas,* or foremen, shook awake anyone who tried to catch a few extra moments of sleep.

The workers then marched to the fields to begin a 10-hour work-day in the tropical sun. Sugarcane was the primary product of the plantations. During the months when the cane grew, laborers with hoes hacked weeds from the cane rows, wrapping wet cloths around their faces to keep from breathing the red dust of the soil. At harvest time, the razor-sharp leaves of the plants had to be stripped off by hand before the canes were cut and tied into bundles. Then work be-gan in the "sugar house," where the canes were crushed to release the greenish, foul-smelling juice that was turned into sugar.

Though a minority of Japanese immigrants were women, some ac-companied their husbands to Hawaii and worked in the fields alongside them. Some of these women earned extra money by washing, cooking, and sewing.

The Japanese came prepared for hard work, but they resented the cruel and impersonal way they were treated. Workers had to wear a *bango,* a brass tag with an identi-fication number. The lunas always called them by number, not by name, and swung a whip at anyone who worked too slowly. Workers could be fined for such offenses as breaking a tool or being late for work. If a laborer missed a day due to illness, he or she had to make it up with two extra days' work. When workers' contracts were sold to another plantation, they were abruptly shipped off to their new employer. To many Japanese, this system seemed like slavery. In addi-tion, they received lower pay than the Portuguese and Puerto Rican laborers for performing the same work.

In 1900, the Hawaiian Islands became a territory of the United States. The labor-contract system was illegal under U.S. law, and now the 60,000 Japanese in Ha-waii became free to negotiate their own terms of employment. How-ever, the owners of the sugar plantations made secret agreements among themselves to keep wages low. If a worker left his plantation without permission, no other em-ployer would hire him.

Even so, the Japanese, who by 1900 formed the largest single eth-nic group in Hawaii, started to organize labor unions. In May 1909, about 7,000 Japanese labor-ers in the Higher Wage Association went on strike to demand pay equal to that of Portuguese and Puerto Rican workers. In retalia-tion, the plantation owners ejected strikers and their families from their homes, and leaders of the as-sociation were arrested. The strike was called off in August, though the planters soon equalized the pay system.

In December 1919, the Federa-tion of Japanese Labor (FJL) was formed. It demanded an increase in the minimum plantation wage from 77¢ to $1.25 a day for men, and from 58¢ to 95¢ a day for women. In addition, the FJL asked for an eight-hour workday, eight weeks of paid maternity leave for women, and improved health care. After the owners turned down these demands, a strike began in January 1920. The owners ruth-lessly tried to break it, evicting some 12,000 men, women, and children from plantation housing and bringing in nonunion laborers.

The islands' newspapers came down strongly on the side of the owners. The Honolulu *Star-Bulletin* asked, "Is control of this [industry] of Hawaii to remain in the hands of Anglo-Saxons or is it to pass into those of alien Japanese agitators?" The strike collapsed on July 1, but in its aftermath many Issei and Nisei workers left the plantations to find other jobs.

Some were employed on planta-tions that had been started by prosperous members of the Japa-nese-Hawaiian community. By 1914, Japanese-owned plantations were producing about 80 percent of the coffee beans and 50 percent of the pineapples in Hawaii.

Issei were also pioneers in the Hawaiian fishing industry. By

1914, five large-scale Japanese-owned fishing companies were operating in Hawaii, as well as several boat-building and fish-processing firms.

The immigrants who went to the mainland United States faced problems of other kinds. The would-be students of the 1880s and 1890s took jobs as domestic servants while attending classes at night. The chores required in an American home were completely foreign to their experience. The poet Yone Noguchi recalled: "Even a stove was a mystery to us. One of my friends endeavored to make a fire by burning the kindling in the oven....One fellow terrified the lady when he began to take off his shoes, and even his trousers, before scrubbing the floor....It was natural enough for him, since he...was afraid he might spoil them."

Though it was illegal to bring in workers who had already signed labor contracts, recruiting agents simply signed up immigrants as they left the ships. Since most Japanese immigrants did not speak English, they were at the mercy of unscrupulous contractors whose promises of high wages and good living conditions were often empty ones. By the time an immigrant found out the truth, he was under contract in an isolated mining town, a logging camp, or on a railroad work gang.

Railroads, mining and logging companies, and fish canneries used English-speaking Japanese "bosses" to supervise their Japanese laborers. Some of these bosses formed their own companies and became labor contractors themselves.

The majority of Japanese immigrants on the mainland found their first jobs as migrant farmworkers (called *buranke-katsugi*—"people who shouldered blankets"). Living in railroad cars, they moved from place to place, stopping wherever a crop was being harvested, from southern California's Imperial Valley to the orchards in Washington State.

Many dreamed of starting their own farms—one reason why many Japanese immigrants stayed in California, where land was plenti-

The contract labor system prohibited plantation workers in Hawaii from seeking other jobs or leaving the islands before their contracts expired.

ful. There were four ways that a migrant farmworker could move up the ladder to farm ownership. First was to sign a contract with a landowner, agreeing to plant and harvest a crop in return for a fee. This did not require much capital, for usually the landowner supplied seed, tools, and fertilizer. Another way was sharecropping, in which the farmer received a percentage of the profits, instead of a fee, when the crop was sold.

A third way was to lease the land, keeping all the profits. Finally, a farmer could purchase land outright. There was more risk in these last two methods, for an immigrant might have to obtain credit from merchants or loans from banks to get through the year. If the crop failed, he could lose everything.

Yet many succeeded. By 1910, Japanese Americans farmed almost 200,000 acres of land in California, leasing 89,000 acres and owning 17,000. Many of these acres were barren wasteland before Issei farmers, accustomed to working every inch of scarce farmland at home, reclaimed it for agriculture.

Though they owned only a tiny percentage of California's 28 million acres of farmland, Japanese led the way in growing certain kinds of crops. The head of the Japanese Agricultural Association of California stated in 1918 that 80 to 90 percent of California's strawberries, asparagus, celery, and tomatoes were grown by Japanese.

However, the very success of the Japanese American farmers caused jealousy and fear.

Anti-Japanese prejudice was strongest in California. In 1913 the state legislature passed the Alien Land Act, which prohibited "aliens ineligible for citizenship" from purchasing land or leasing it for a period longer than three years. Aliens who already owned land could continue to hold it, but they could not sell it to other aliens or even leave it as an inheritance to other aliens.

The Japanese Americans in California used a variety of ways to get around the law. Some registered their land in the names of their children, who were American citizens by birth and hence exempt from the law. Others joined together to form companies that held title to their land.

In 1920, California tightened the restrictions, forbidding Japanese immigrants from leasing land or sharecropping. The intention was to force them to the lowest level of farm work, as migrant laborers. Other states—Washington, Arizona, New Mexico, Oregon, Montana, Idaho, and Texas—passed similar laws. The Japanese Association, formed in 1908 by representatives from many Japanese American communities, brought legal challenges against these laws, but the U.S. Supreme Court eventually upheld the state restrictions.

Japanese Americans faced other kinds of prejudice and discrimination. In general, the mainstream American labor movement refused to allow Asian Americans as members. In 1903, Japanese and Mexican sugar-beet workers in Oxnard, California, formed a labor union and went on strike when their demand for higher wages were on met. Samuel Gompers, the head of the American Federation of Labor, agreed to issue a charter to the struggling union—but only if it expelled its Japanese members. The Mexican American secretary of the union refused to betray his Japanese "brothers," and without the support of the AFL the Japanese-Mexican Labor Organization died.

After the Japanese section of San Francisco was destroyed in the great earthquake that devastated the city in 1906, Japanese families moved into other areas of the city. They met resistance from whites who did not want Asians living near them. That fall, when Japanese children sought to attend local public schools, the San Francisco school board ordered all of them transferred to the "Oriental school" in Chinatown.

The segregated school became an international issue when the Japanese government protested.

Three Issei lumberjacks at Winans Lumber Camp in Dee, Oregon, in 1908. Some railroad laborers found jobs like this in towns along the tracks after the railroads were built.

President Theodore Roosevelt met with California's congressional delegation and the mayor of San Francisco to hammer out a solution. The school board partially backed down; in return Roosevelt promised to seek ways to limit Japanese immigration. A man of his word, he negotiated the Gentlemen's Agreement the following year.

Politicians and newspapers fanned the fire of anti-Japanese sentiment. Mayor James D. Phelan of San Francisco declared in 1900 that "Japanese are not...the stuff of which American citizens can be made." Anti-Japanese groups such as the Asiatic Exclusion League and the Native Sons of the Golden West charged that Japanese laborers took jobs from American citizens because they could live on less money than white people.

Boycotts were organized against Japanese shops and businesses; slogans such as "Get Out Jap" were painted on their homes and stores. Sometimes prejudice took violent forms. In July 1921, in Turlock, California, mobs of white men rounded up Japanese laborers, put them on trucks and railroad cars, and warned them that if they returned they would be lynched.

The growing number of Nisei children continued to arouse hostility. In 1920, a U.S. senator from California proposed a constitutional amendment to deny citizenship even to American-born children of Asian immigrants. Though this amendment failed, Congress passed the Cable Act in 1922. It deprived female Americans of their citizenship if they married "an alien ineligible for citizenship." The act was directed against Nisei women who married Issei men but was sometimes applied even to white women who married Issei.

The passage of the 1924 immigration law, which barred all future immigration from Japan, was a shock to the Issei. They viewed it as an insult, a denial that they had been patriotic and valuable residents of their adopted land. It meant that the U.S. government supported the prejudice against them.

PLANTATION WORK

Shoshichi and Chika Saka emigrated to Hawaii from Japan in 1885 to work on a sugar plantation. Their daughter, Raku Saka Morimoto, recalled what her parents said about those days.

My parents were sent to Kekaha, Kauai and they worked there for three years. You know, Chinese, they used to have a queue, long hair. [The] *luna*, the overseer, when he's not pleased with their work, he just got hold of the hair, wind it around his palm, and just drag them here and there. And he [father] said, oh, it's so pitiful to see the Chinese almost crying and asking to let them go. But he said, "We Japanese are lucky because our hair is so short." (Laughs.)

But their treatment was terrible, you know. They were contract labor by name, but they were actually like slaves. So, they got together and said, "Well, let's write a letter to Japanese consul. Tell [him] to come over and talk to the manager, and change this bad situation." They wrote so many times, but consul didn't come. So, they said, "Well, we better send somebody up with the petition and get the consul to come over." But if a man stays away from work, he has to pay six dollars and a half or six dollars fine. They were getting only nine dollars a month, working ten hours a day. Finally, they asked my mother to [go] over to get the Japanese consul. So, my mother [went]. I was just thinking, my mother must have been very brave woman (chuckles) for her small size, because she didn't know anybody in Honolulu.

Since the consul doesn't make a move, she has to wait, because she was told by the Japanese in Kekaha not to come back all by herself but "bring the consul with you." I don't know exactly how long [it took], but the consul went with her to Kekaha. He asked for complaints, you know, of [the] Japanese people about the situation. [Then] he said, "Well, you have a house free, water free, wood free. And what more do you want?" So, he was not any help to the Japanese people.

The Japanese were very angry. Some of them are so disappointed. They said, "Japanese government sent the consul here to protect us, but he doesn't protect us at all." One man was so angry, he said, "If I kill anybody, well, I'm going to lose my life, too. So, I'm going to kill the consul." He knew where the consul was going, you see, from one plantation to the other plantation. And [the consul] has to pass a lonely place. [When] the consul was passing there on a buggy, [the man] jumped out [from] behind the bush and hold onto the horse bridle. The horse jumped up, and the bridle gave way. The consul whipped

These Japanese contract laborers on a Hawaiian sugar plantation around 1890 were photographed with their *bangos,* or identification numbers.

Although Hawaii made school attendance mandatory for children up to the age of 15, many worked to help support their families. These boys tend the crops on a farm in Oahu.

the horse, let the horse run as fast as he could, and went to the other camp, you see. So, the consul was saved.

Baishiro Tamashiro went to Hawaii from Okinawa in 1906. Seventy years later, he recalled his hard times in the cane fields.

I went to Lihue because the plantation there did not have enough men.... We started work the next day. We got *bango* (numbers). For one week new men worked separately. Since we used knives, our hands were blistered. They sure hurt! Fourteen or fifteen of us. We worked together. When we got used to the work we worked among 200 *kachi kane* (cut cane) men.

It sure was hard work. We had no time to rest. We worked like machines. For 200 of us workers, there were seven or eight *luna*s and above them was a field boss on a horse. We were watched constantly. They would not give us good knives. After work they just threw the knives around. If I didn't go to work early enough the good knives were all gone. Only small or dull knives were left. They were not sharp enough. In those days I was just 19 years old, healthy and strong.

At Lihue Plantation they were burning cane, and soot was all over my face.... We had no time to rest. "Boy, your knife does not cut. Show it to me," a *luna* would say and exchanged it with his sharpened knife. Even after going to the bathroom, I had to rush and catch up with them because the *luna* would say, "Go ahead, go ahead."...

A luna, or overseer, mounted on a horse, supervises Japanese women plantation workers in Hawaii. A luna sometimes whipped those who did not work hard enough.

As Others Saw Them

On February 10, 1885, the Daily Pacific Commercial Advertiser, *a Hawaiian newspaper, described a group of new immigrants from Japan:*

The first thing that attracts the attention of the visitor to the depot is the fairness of the skins of the immigrants....Many of them, the women especially, are actually white, and they are all very clean.... The Japs mount themselves on pieces of wood cut rudely into the semblance of a shoe sole....

Cooking was going on, the food being in vessels of quaint and pretty shape and design placed over fire kindled in holes dug in the soft sand. These people eat no meat, their diet consisting almost entirely of fish, with which they are abundantly supplied. Rice is with them an important article of food and they like all kinds of vegetables. They cook in messes, and there is the usual amount of bustle about the numerous fires, that is inseparable from the preparing of food the world over....

They bathe, dress, and sleep in quiet, and everything seem to show that they will rapidly become domesticated here.

Workers at a sugarcane plantation at Puunene, Maui, Hawaii. Such workers earned about $16 a month. After the United States annexed Hawaii in 1898, many Japanese laborers started to leave the islands for the mainland, where wages were higher.

The hardest plantations to work for were Lihue and Makaweli. The others were not as bad. Makaweli was the worst of them all.

Makaweli had the *poho* ("out of luck") system. When you didn't cut well they would say, "You *poho*" and would subtract 50 cents.... If the *poho* happened many times you lost out a lot. They were making a lot of money that way.

In cutting cane when you don't cut from the root the *luna* will come and say *poho*. When the *luna* saw that there was a little left of the cane or some weeds around, he would say *poho* again. They have even taken "Five dollars!" from me that way. When I was paid, I cried. My job at that time was picking the leftover cane. After my work was done, there was one cane left behind. The *luna* found that and said, "You *poho*." I had seen that, but I did not cut it since it was too small. Since I could speak a bit of English, I told the *luna*, "Are you going to *poho* over such a minor thing?" I argued with him. Yeah. Then he said five dollars *poho*. Although *poho* is 50 cents the *luna* had taken five dollars from me. I was so angry that I wanted to knock him down, but I decided not to be foolish enough to fight over such small money. *Poho* here and *poho* there and I think the Portuguese boss must have had a lot of money. That was an awful place.

Chinzen Kinjo, who came to Hawaii in the early years of the 20th century, described the cruelty of the lunas.

The life on Ewa Plantation was very hard; getting up at 4 A.M., breakfast at 5, starting to work at 6, and working all day under the blazing sun. We worked like horses, moving mechanically under the whipping hands of the luna. There was no such thing as human sentiment. At night, instead of a sweet dream of my wife and child left in Okinawa, I was wakened up frightened by the nightmare of being whipped by the luna. Because of the perpetual fear of this unbearable whipping, some other workers committed suicide by hanging or jumping in front of the on-coming train....

There was no one who wasn't whipped. Once when the luna whipped me by taking me for someone else, I was really mad and all the anger which had hitherto been suppressed in me exploded and I challenged him with Karate (Okinawan art of self-defense). Since the luna was a big man, a six-footer, it wasn't easy for me. But finally, I threw him to the ground. I could have kicked him to unconsciousness. There was a crowd surrounding us. Some cheered me, waving cane knives, shouting, "Kinjo, go ahead, go ahead!" The others shouted, "Beat him up; finish him!" I was at the point of jumping at him, risking my whole life in that one blow. Right at that moment, a Big Luna (superior overseer) came and calmed me down, saying, "Wait, wait; I will fix everything all right." Thus, the incident ended short of serious consequences. We wanted revenge even to the point of committing murder. You can understand how brutally the laborers of early years were treated.

Haruno Nunogawa Sato, who emigrated to Hawaii from Japan in 1915, when she was 10, started working in the cane fields when she was 13.

In dressing for work in the sugar cane fields, our biggest worry was to keep out the centipedes and other things from crawling inside. The clothes also had to protect us from the irritating fuzz on the sugar cane and the sharp edges of the leaves.

This is how I dressed for work: 1) put on long tight cotton pants. 2) I put on my tabis [thick socks] and tightened the drawstring. 3) I firmly wound a kyahan (knee to ankle leg wrapping) and tied it to keep the centipedes from crawling between the pants bottom and the tabis. 4) I put on my long sleeved shirt, and 5) I put on my short striped cotton *hakama* (skirt) which was about an inch or two below the knee. 6) I wrapped an *obi* [waistband] firmly around my waist so that nothing could creep in between my shirt and skirt. Sometimes in unwrapping the *obi*, we found centipedes and other insects. 7) I tied on the *te oi* (arm cover which extended from my finger joints to the elbow) to keep bugs out of my sleeves and to prevent the back of the hands from getting cut. I did not wear gloves. 8) I then covered my head with a white muslin cloth, put on my *papale* (hat) and put a pin through the hat to hold everything down. The papale styles differed from plantation to plantation. Some had wide brims while others were like bonnets. Because we wanted to keep our complexion fair and our faces from being scratched by the sharp leaves, we covered our faces with a man's handkerchief when we worked. Only our eyes were exposed. Nowadays, they wear goggles.

Two workers collect chopped sugarcane. The man at left is wearing protective clothing and headgear that were traditionally used by farm workers in Japan.

After fulfilling their labor contracts, some Japanese in Hawaii went into vegetable farming or raised poultry or opened stores. This woman offers vegetables for sale on Oahu around 1925.

A steam engine draws a cane car that takes the chopped sugarcane to a mill. Another machine (at front) tills the soil. Despite the development of mechanized farm equipment, cutting the cane itself required hand labor.

Tomonosuke Takahashi was 90 when he was interviewed in 1974 about the life of a bachelor laborer in Hawaii.

I first arrived in Honolulu on the *Lennox* on September 15, 1899.... I was sent to Kealia, Kaua'i at $15.00 per month.... Seven of us stayed in one room in the *nagaya* (long house). At first we spread *goza* (straw mats) on the floor to sleep. Then I bought a straw bed for 50 cents at the company store. The cotton pants and *yukata* (cotton kimono) which I had brought with me were not suitable for the fields so I bought a pair of *tabis* (socks) at 25¢ and *ahina* (denim) pants and shirt at $1.50 on credit. The purchases were deducted from my pay.

Mine Sekine Omiya went to Hawaii as a picture bride. She remembered the ride to her new home. She saw a beautiful house on a hill, but the horse-drawn buggy made its way on a dirt road to a row of shacks. Here she had to make a home for herself and her new husband, which required much hard work.

Washing clothes was a whole day job on Sundays. What we did was build a fire outside under a 5-gallon kerosene can filled with soapy water. We would boil the dirty clothes...the brown soap was really strong those days...then take the clothes out and beat them to get the dirt out. I used to hang our clothes out for several days because it took so long to dry.

Some women took in washing and ironing for the single men, instead of working in the fields. But if a woman delivered the laundry and stayed to talk a while, there were all kinds of rumors so many of us didn't like doing laundry for the bachelors...the single men.

At age 86, Robert Yasui recalled helping his father, who had lost an arm in an accident and was given the job of maintaining the furos, *or community baths, on the plantation.*

As kids we helped my father run the furos which were heated with firewood. Every Saturday and Sunday, we had to saw long keawe [tree] stumps for the week. Later, we switched to charcoal. The furo was open from 2 to 8 P.M. on a first come, first served basis. The cost was 35 cents for single people and 60 cents for a family. The furo was one big, huge bathtub, like a shallow swimming pool, which was partitioned to separate men from women, but the kids swam back and forth under it.

To the Japanese a hot bath was a daily must because being clean was very important. Sitting on stools, people first scrubbed themselves with a long soapy washcloth and then rinsed themselves thoroughly before stepping into the steaming hot water to relax.

Osame Nagata Manago went to Hawaii in 1913 as a picture bride. She described work at a coffee mill in Kona, on the Big Island of Hawaii.

Awoman came and asked if I'd like to sort coffee beans at Napoopoo for the Captain Cook Coffee Company.... So I went with two other women—*obasan-tachi* [aunties or matrons]. It was quite a long walk. I used to leave about seven o'clock in the morning, carrying my year-old baby on my back. I would fix *dango*, dumplings, for him and a *bento* [lunch] for myself....

We used to get thirty-five cents for sorting a bag full of coffee beans, some of which were squashed or split in half, or crumbled, and so on. It was thirty-five cents for one bag sorted. I could hardly do two bags. When the boss found one bad coffee bean in a finished bag, I had to do it all over again, emptying the bag. So I ended up working over one bag twice, when I could have worked on two. It was really miserable at times like that. But the three of us used to comfort each other in our hard work.... And it was only seventy cents a day, not to mention the trouble I had—the kids and the long walk. Finally, people told us that we three women should quit. So we all did.

These Japanese women wear hanahana *(work) outfits. The headgear was designed for protection from the sun. Long-sleeved shirts, tight leg wrappings, and obis, or sashes, were all intended to keep centipedes and other insects away from the body. Most of the workers who chopped the sugarcane also wore gloves.*

This Japanese-owned Hawaiian store catered to the needs of plantation workers by selling tofu *(bean curd),* noodles, rice, and fish cakes. Other Japanese entrepreneurs opened furos, *the traditional hot communal baths.*

OFF THE PLANTATION

When Kame Komatsu was more than 100 years old, she recalled the days in 1913–14, after she moved with her husband and new baby to their own small farm in what is today Honolulu.

Kapiolani Boulevard, as it intersects with King Street, was then a river where Manoa and Palolo streams met. Beyond were rice paddies, taro patches, and pig and duck farms. There were also banana groves and grape orchards. In the stream were eels, about a foot long. Although they were ugly and smelled of mud, they were tasty. The children also caught *namazu*—catfish—and these were delicious.

We raised chickens and the chickens laid eggs well. So we had eggs morning, noon and night. For lunch I would make *musubi* and fry some eggs for the children. For dinner, I would cook vegetables with eggs.

We got a piglet and raised it with leftovers from the kitchen, such as potato, carrot and cucumber skins, the outer leaves of cabbage, and things like that. Sometimes we boiled all the leftovers in the slop bucket on the charcoal that remained from cooking the rice. The pigs ate the food raw or cooked.

Some Japanese plantation workers saved up enough money to open their own businesses. Tokusuke Oshiro, who went to Hawaii as a child in 1915, recalled the struggle he and his wife had in establishing their little shop.

Right then [1940], a friend of mine had a *tofu* (bean curd) shop which he was going to quit. So, I took over the business. I got up around 1:00 or 1:30 A.M. In the morning I had coffee around 5 o'clock and had no lunch.... When I would drive past a small store, I would stop and have a Coca-Cola. I didn't have time to eat and in the end I got a stomach ailment. I was very skinny—only 110 pounds.... It was 4:30 or 5:00 P.M. when I got back home....

My wife and I made the *tofu* and I would go out to sell it. I would sell my *tofu* to restaurants as well as to camps. The farthest I went to sell was Olaa's Juyonri—the camp at the 14 mile marker in Olaa. I had regular customers who knew the days that I would come. So when I honked my horn, people would come out with container in hand....

Soybeans were cheap then, about $3.50 for 100 pounds. *Tofu* was cheap too; five cents was the price. We also sold *aburage* (fried bean curd) to *sushi* (vinegared rice) shops. I remember that there was a man Mr. Oki who made lots of *sushi.*

In 1916, Osame Nagata Manago and her husband opened a coffee shop. It grew over the years into the Manago Hotel, which is still operated by their son. Years later, she recalled its beginnings.

My husband bought a house in which coffee beans used to be dried. He paid ninety dollars for it. We remodeled the house, dividing it into two parts, one for our bedroom, the other with a sink and table for making and selling *udon* [noodles]. We bought a tiny stove, I can't remember exactly how much my husband paid for it, but I think it was some thirty or forty dollars. That's how we started.

We baked bread, about ten loaves a day sometimes, and we served *udon* and coffee. We used to calculate our profits, which were two to three dollars at the end of each day.... Since we didn't have gas or electricity then, we used lamps. And, we needed firewood for the stove. So both of us had to work hard. Meanwhile, our bread sold well. We used to sell out all ten loaves in one day. We served two slices of bread with jam, since we didn't have butter, with a cup of coffee. Even *udon*, of the ten or twenty servings we made, all would be sold....

Above our houselot there used to be a large Paris Hotel. People would come to Kona to sell all sorts of things but their drivers couldn't stay with them at that hotel. Since they didn't have any place to stay, they asked me if they could stay at our shop for a cheap price. So we bought small single beds and put them in the extra space we had, and started letting those drivers stay. That's how we first started the Manago Hotel, back in 1917.

Usaburo Katamoto first went to Hawaii as a 13-year-old boy. Like his father before him, he became a boat builder. In 1978, two years before his death, he described his work.

For the fishermen, we build the boat and then we notify after we finish 'em. And they figured we make a boat strong enough. It's very seldom we lost a boat at sea. The government used to send the inspector to check, you know, but they pretty easy on us. They measure, eh? This boat is so-and-so capacity, tonnage, you know, under certain class. And they tell us what to do....

Every time we fix a boat or build one, we make a trial run. Try the engine, power plant, and boat. And we used to take them out Diamond Head, or farther out. A five-, six-hour trial run. We throw out a line and sometimes we catch fish....

Later, when the owners launch their boat, it's customary, they celebrate even if they don't have any money. All the friends do it for them anyway, you know. They used bamboo from Manoa valley to put up flags on the new boat for good luck. And, they start make *mochi,* rice cake, eh. They throw that for good luck. Sometimes they put prizes in the cake itself. They get good prizes. Was quite a few celebrations they used to have and usually they put up a tent and throw big party. And, we builders, they throw us in the water. So I couldn't afford to get any good watch. We always get thrown in.

Sewing clothes was one occupation open to Japanese women who had completed their labor contracts. They could do the work at home or in workshops like this one in Honolulu.

55

All the Japanese servants in this picture were employed in the large house at upper right, which was probably the home of an American plantation owner who grew rich from the sugar-cane industry in Hawaii.

Restaurant workers in Idaho in the early 20th century. The success of earlier Chinese immigrants in the restaurant business prompted some Japanese to try it.

STUDENTS AND LABORERS

Many of the young Japanese men who came to the United States in the 1880s and 1890s were students looking for work to pay for their education. The most common job these student-laborers found was as a domestic servant. Their employers called them "schoolboys." The following is an anonymous account by one such servant, from an interview conducted in 1915.

The place where I got to work in the first time was a boarding house. My duties were to peel potatoes, wash the dishes, a few laundry work, and also I was expected to do whatever mistress, waitress and cook has told me.

When I first entered the kitchen wearing a white apron what an uncomfortable and mortifying feeling I experienced. I thought I shall never be able to proceed with the work. I felt as if I am pressed down on my shoulder with loaded tons of weight. My heart palpitates. I did not know what I am and what to say. I stood by the door of kitchen motionless like a stone, with a dumbfounded silence. The cook gave me a scornful look and said nothing....

Whistling up the courage I started to work. The work being entirely new and also such an unaccustomed one, I felt exceedingly unpleasant and hard. Sonorous voice from the cook of my slowness in peeling potatoes often vibrated.... The waitress occasionally called out for the butter plates and saucers at the top of her displeasing voice. Frequently the words "Hurry up!" were added. I always noticed her lips [moving] rather than hands. The proprietor, an old lady, painstakingly taught me to work how. Almost always [beginning with] the phrase "I show you" and ending "Did you understand?" The words were so prominently sounded; finally made me tired of it and...grew hated to hear of it.... Thus I have been working almost all the time from 5:30 A.M. to 9 P.M. When I got through the day's work I was tired.

Yoshio Markino worked as a servant in a private home in San Francisco, an experience he found humiliating.

I was told there was one job as a "school-boy" in Sutter Street near Steiner Street. First thing I had to do was to buy a white coat and apron. Some Japanese lent me the money for that. Then he took me to the house. He settled my wages with the "ma'am"—one dollar and half a week.

Immediately the ma'am demanded me to scrub the kitchen floor. I took one hour to finish. Then I had to wash windows. That was very difficult job for me. Three windows for another hour! She said "You are slow worker, but you do everything so neat. Never mind; you will learn by and by. I like you very much."

In the evening her husband, sons, and daughters came back. The whole family was eight in number. The ma'am taught me how to cook.

She asked me if my name was "Charlie." I said, "Yes, ma'am." At the dinner-table, she called, "Charlie, Charlie." But by that time I had quite forgotten that "Charlie" was my own name; so I did not answer. I was sitting on the kitchen chair and thinking what a change of life it was. The ma'am came into the kitchen and was so furious! It was such a hard work for me to wash up all dishes, pans, glasses, etc., after dinner. When I went into the dining room to put all silvers on sideboard, I saw the reflection of myself on the looking glass. In a white coat and apron! I could not control my feelings. The tears so freely flowed out from my eyes, and I buried my face with my both arms.

Yone Noguchi, a poet, went to San Francisco in 1893 as a student laborer. He described his job delivering the Japanese American newspaper Soko Shimbun.

The (Patriotic) League was then publishing a daily paper called the *Soko Shimbun...*, for which I was engaged as a carrier; the paper had only a circulation of not over two hundred. I did not enter into any talk about payment; I soon discovered it was perfectly useless when we hardly knew how to get dinner every day. You can imagine how difficult it was for five or six people to make a living out of a circulation of two hundred.... By turns, we used to get up and build a fire and prepare big pancakes...with no egg or milk, just with water.

Japanese-language newspapers were very popular in Japanese American communities. Washizu Bunzo worked for the Shin Sekai, *which was established in 1894.*

Among those who lived in San Francisco, the majority were students. Cobblers, laundrymen, and a few store operators had families who numbered less than fifty. Since those scattered in rural areas were either railroad laborers or other transients, they did not subscribe to newspapers.... The newspapers...were only read by the students in San Francisco. Because the Japanese community was not cohesive, they were distributed to people of like mind rather than read by all classes....

The life of newspapermen...was wretched. It was commonplace for publishers to be lithographers and delivery boys. Three meals a day were impossible. The *Soko Shimbun* [*San Francisco News*], which took pride in being the oldest newspaper, had a broken-down stove in the kitchen (an old one worth five dollars). The staff ate biscuits as hard as rocks with no butter.... If they weren't on the verge of starvation, the food was inedible.

A 19th-century guide for Japanese student-laborers published this model conversation to help potential schoolboys both with English and interview techniques:

Japanese: Good-morning; Is this Mrs. Smith's house?

Householdhead: Yes, where you come from?

Japanese: I came from Japanese Mission, they told me that you want school boy.

Householdhead: Yes, just come in and sit down there. Can you speak English?

Japanese: Yes, Madam, I can talk some.

Householdhead: Do you know how to work?

Japanese: I understand house-work, but I don't know anything about cooking.

Householdhead: O, that's very easy; only make coffee, cook mush, and peel potatoes, that's all.

Japanese: Will you teach me?

Householdhead: Yes, I'll show you.

Japanese: What time shall I get up?

Householdhead: Six o'clock; then wash the front steps.

Japanese: All right, madam.

Householdhead: How much wages you want a week.

Japanese: Let me see; and how many people in your family?

Householdhead: Only three, and I have very nice room for you.

Japanese: Will you, please, show me the room. Well, then give me a dollar and a half a week, and I wish to go out at half past eight in the morning, and come home at four in the afternoon.

Householdhead: Yes, and what is your name?

Japanese: My name is Frank.

Householdhead: All right, Frank, you work from to-day.

Japanese: Yes, madam, I will come to-day at four o'clock in the after-noon. Good-day.

As Others Saw Them

H. A. Millis was the author of a book entitled The Japanese Problem in the United States, *which was published in 1915. He wrote about Japanese railroad workers:*

The Japanese found favor with the roadmasters and foremen because of their efficiency, and their good behavior in camp. On the whole they proved to be better workmen than any other of the immigrant races, the Mexican excepted, and the absence of brawls in camp set them in strong contrast to certain other competing races. So...the rate of wages of Japanese advanced more rapidly than that of other races.

FINDING A JOB

Because it was illegal for contract laborers to enter the United States, newly arrived immigrants from Japan had to find their own jobs. Sometimes friends or relatives helped, but often the newcomers were recruited by work agencies, some of them Japanese. Taro Yoshitake recalled his adventures after being signed up to work on a railroad.

When I first arrived in Seattle in February, 1902, I was solicited by Tobo [a Japanese work agency]. Along with four other fellows, aged from 18 to 21, I was to go to the job site, which was "300 miles from Seattle." The Tobo company man told us, "Brothers, stay in the train until a Japanese comes to you and says to get off." So we obeyed him, staying in the train all of one night, and around noon the next day a Japanese came to us and said, "You fellows from Seattle get off here."

We were suspicious that it was too far for 300 miles, and so I asked him where we were. He answered that it was Harbor, Montana, 1000 miles from Seattle, and we were astonished. Our job was section work, at 85¢ per day for 10 hours. Four men made one group and stayed in one shack. Spreading blankets on the hay, we went to sleep. We took turns cooking. The menu was *miso* soup, *bottera* [pancakes], and dumpling soup, and we bought eggs from the neighboring farmer at 15¢ a dozen. We could also eat beef. Now and then we found a

Railroad workers at a camp in the Northwest. In 1906, the year before the Gentleman's Agreement halted male Japanese immigration, about one out of every three Issei in the mainland United States worked for railroad companies.

dead cow run over by a train and we were never short of meat. But unfortunately, we didn't know how to cook, so when we found such a cow we only used the cheap groin sections and boiled them. I don't know why, but the way it bubbled and foamed, it gave us the creeps....

We checked up and down the line for 20 miles by handcar, and if there was some accident, we had to go, whether it was day or night. It was hard work. Among the four of us, one man, aged 30...became night-blind and at night his legs got cramps and he screamed out, "Ouch, ouch!" I also had legs cramps—the work was that hard.

Izo Kojima recalled working on a railroad that served a sawmill near Portland, Oregon, around 1920.

My job was to replace old ties or repair crooked rails. They used a steam-powered cable to bring down the logs from the mountains. It was a dynamic scene—the huge cable stretched across the valleys from mountain to mountain, on which hung logs that weighed tons. The food, which came from Furuya Company, and the mail, all depended on the locomotives in the mountains.

The camp consisted of barracks, in each of which four or five men lived together. The beds were wooden box-style and the mattresses were straw stuffed into canvas. At night if you moved around in your sleep you made a crackling sound. Under the oil lamp I tried to read lecture notes from middle school which I got from Japan, and tried to study English, but among us there was a guy who was very good at talking...so I just couldn't concentrate on mere books.

I made $4.50 a day for eight hours of labor. The food expense was $15 a month, and in addition we each paid $2.50 for the woman cook. Breakfast was *tofu* in *miso* soup, pickles and rice. We carried a sack lunch with meat or eggs. Sometimes in the lunch sack there was a can of sardines. At lunchtime the tea boy made Japanese tea. At noon we circled around a fire, toasted our bread on the end of a long stick and ate it. I can never forget the taste of it even now.

Japanese immigrants also found work in mines in the western states. Hyoza Kumagai worked in a coal mine in Rock Springs, Wyoming, when he was 14. He recalled that workers of different nationalities lived in separate camps.

People of over 40 different nationalities were working in the mines, but southern Europeans were most numerous. [Besides the Japanese], there was also an Italian camp and a Greek camp, but there were almost no camps of more than 40 or 50 people because, unlike the Japanese, European workers did not like group living. The 200 to 300 Japanese who lived together were consdered unusual.

The Caucasian miners went to their place of work at 7:00 in the morning by pit train (six men in each car). The Japanese miners got up at 2:00 A.M., ate their breakfast, and left home at

Small Japanese American communities grew along the railroad lines in the Northwest. Several women and a baby appear in this picture of a logging camp in Nehalem, Oregon, in the 1890s—their presence indicates that a permanent community was taking root.

Japanese American loggers at an Oregon camp around 1908. Japanese who were recruited to cut timber in the Hood River Valley of Oregon stayed to plant apple and pear orchards on the cleared land.

Employees of a fish cannery at Terminal Island, California, in the early 20th century. They cut up the fish, cooked it, and then canned it.

2:45. They fastened to their waist 3 *go* (1 *go* = .384 pint) of lamp oil, in their left hand they carried a lunch box, and on their right shoulder a pickax. They walked along the mine railroad track for three or four miles to the mouth of the pit, reaching their place of work about 5:00 A.M. The day ended when they returned by pit train, leaving at 5:30 P.M....

Half the 272 people living in the Jap camp took their meals at a boarding house managed by the boss. The remainder ate at any of four other places in the camp....

Produce—Chinese cabbage, onions, Japanese radishes, and soybeans—was ordered from a Chinese peddler named Chan who came by the camp twice a week. The members bought fish—tuna, sea bass, sardines, and other varieties—from Okano Tsuruji's shop in town and had meat and beverages delivered from the company store. They ate the fish cooked Japanese-style or raw as sashimi. At New Year's, one group paid a great sum of money to purchase red snapper from a fish market in Galveston, Texas.

Since camp life was brutal, drinking and gambling were almost the only pleasures, and the sounds of pistols were heard every night. There were simpler pleasures as well. On summer evenings, for example, some 50 or 60 people gathered on a gentle slope near the camp to listen as one of their number read aloud from old adventure tales. Almost no one wrote home, since they would have had to write YOKOHAMA, JAPAN on the envelope. It cost a sum of money to have one of the few people who could write English perform this service.

Fishing and gathering shellfish were familiar occupations to many of the Japanese immigrants. Tonoyo Fujita, who emigrated to the United States at the age of 16 in 1924, just before the ban on Asian immigration, married an Issei who worked in a sawmill. However, circumstances forced them to take up oystering.

In the Depression period around 1930 we lost money because the Furuya bank was closed and the sawmill was to be closed too, so we moved into the oyster business. Ikko

Japanese women in a California fruit-processing plant around 1910. They sorted the fruit and then boxed it for shipping.

Murakami was growing cranberries at Long Beach, Washington, and he happened to say he would import seed oysters from Matsushima Bay, Japan, and start an oyster farm on a large scale, and so we joined him. There we shucked oysters...and in 1935 we began the Pine Island Oyster Company in Willapa Bay. Since we didn't have citizenship, we borrowed the name of Reverend Murphy for about ten years, to engage in the oyster business....

On the ocean where we worked with the oysters, sometimes miserable accidents occurred. In those days, during the winter Alaska boys frequently came to work in the oyster business. Carrying an oil lantern they went out to the ocean in the deep of the night. The lantern could burn for ten hours. The workers dumped the baskets full of harvested oysters into a flat-bottomed boat. When the tide began to rise, they came back to the mother-boat and returned. Oyster harvesters, if they were not paying close attention, might easily lose their sense of direction, in which case they would be drowned. One night three men were lost in this way.

Minejiro Shibata, who came to the United States from Shizuoka prefecture in 1919 when he was 17, related his experiences in the fishing business in California.

I and a few others saved four or five thousand dollars to build a fishing boat together in 1924. Our boat was among the biggest in those days. We could heap eighty or ninety tons of tuna on the boat. There were fish everywhere then....

We ate fairly well, but though our business was brisk, few fishermen became rich.... We earned more, for we built a bigger boat....

Fishing might look easy when there aren't any fish around, because we just look for them. Once we start fishing, we often stay overnight—that's exhausting and dangerous. In 1928, while I was hanging the net, the end of it was accidentally cut by a rock, and I was caught under the net. I was told that I was unconscious for a half hour. The X-rays showed that I was fine. Some of the others got their legs or arms broken, but I was fine.

During a storm, I was often afraid that the boat wouldn't hold up, but I forgot the fear and hardship as soon as the storm passed. We never threw away fish [to lighten the boat] because of a storm. We wouldn't have given them up even for our lives. Once some Japanese fishermen were fishing with us around an island. We warned them the night before that a storm was coming.... When the storm came, five people were thrown to their deaths on the rocks. We picked up seven others who were lucky enough to be thrown ashore by the waves.

I remember in 1924 a friend of mine came to me on the night before he was to sail. He shook my hand, left, and never came back.

The United States Immigration Commission commented on the exploitation of the Japanese Americans who worked in the Alaskan salmon canneries around 1905.

They [Japanese bosses] secure the men through subagents...who receive a commission of five dollars per man, which is deducted from the wages of the men engaged. An advance is usually made by the packers to the "boss" in the spring.... An extensive stock of eatables is bought, which is destined to be sold at high prices to the men en route. This is made possible by the fact that the food regularly furnished is poor and frequently insufficient in quantity.... The men buy these extra eatables and gamble at tables conducted by subbosses, on credit, their expenditures and losses being deducted from their total earnings for the season. The income of the "boss" is thus obtained from two sources—the sale of goods to the men...and the profits realized from gambling. This income is comparatively large...; frequently, if not generally, amounting to from two thousand to five thousand dollars for the year. It is entirely the result of the exploitation of the wages of Japanese laborers.

Sawmill workers at Barnaston, Washington, in 1911. The daughter of one of the men is at the left of the second row.

Workers at an Alaskan cannery in 1929 start to unload a salmon barge. Because the fish had to be processed as soon as possible after they were netted, the workday could be as long as 20 hours.

During the summer months, some Japanese went north to Alaska to fish for salmon or work in the canneries, as Rev. Masaru Kumata remembered.

S almon fishing in Alaska was done every year for five months, from April to August. Among the Alaska boys, the early birds left Seattle as soon as April began and went directly to the canneries in Alaska.... Most of them put on overalls and hunting caps, and carried a seabag over their shoulders. In the bag...they packed three blankets...a pillow, working clothes and miscellaneous belongings. As far as I know, most of them carried a pistol in their pocket....

Piping a melancholy whistle over the piers of Seattle, the freight boat nosed out toward the north. Though they were all called "Alaska boys," among them were high school and college students, and sometimes old men of sixty or seventy years of age. We were all put into the hold where the strong smell of salmon cakes gripped our noses....

Now as to the work: From 200,000 to 600,000 fish were brought in by the nets at one time. The boys were eagerly awaiting them in the camp. First, the boys who pitch fish threw them in; then the sorters sorted them. As many as 200 salmon per minute came up to the deck via the conveyor belt, their silver scales shining. The sorters, holding hooks in both hands, began their extremely arduous struggle with this multitude of salmon. Since a sorter had to sort 200 per minute, he didn't have a single second to relax. Opening their eyes as wide as plates, the sorters stared at the fish, for experts could tell in a split second, by glancing at a part of the nose or at the shade of the tail, whether the fish was a humpback, a king, a dog salmon, or a sockeye.

The butchers were waiting. In the early days, the cutting off of the heads and splitting of the belly was all done by hand.... It was not so much like men struggling with innumerable fish, as

Teruo Murata leased space in a large store to sell fruit and vegetables in the Los Angeles area. He sent out this greeting card, with his name signed in Japanese characters at upper right and his photo at upper left.

like human maggots wiggling and squirming among swarms of salmon. The scheduled working hours were from 6 A.M. to 6 P.M., but when the salmon didn't come in, everyone just lay around relaxing.

For work like this the income went as high as $85 to $150 a month.... If every cannery boy saved all his precious money earned this way...they could get from $500 to $1,000 together, which was their goal before going back to Japan. But the reality was not according to such a simple calculation. Here is the tragedy of Alaska boys.

In the work camps of the Japanese, gambling was a favorite pastime. It was often encouraged by the boss, who profited the most by it, as Tappei Tsuda told the Japanese writer Hisashi Tsurutani.

When payday came, the boss borrowed a freight car to use as a gambling hall, and four or five professional Japanese gamblers arrived from Seattle. They gambled for two nights or so and then went back to Seattle, leaving almost all the workers swindled out of the month's wages. Of course, whether the workers won or lost, a lot of money went into the pockets of the boss who had backed the operation. Gambling flourished in this way even in the temporary quarters and freight cars of the mountains. It goes without saying that every nice-looking town saloon had a gambling hall in its basement.... When a person saw piles of gold coins stacked up on the table and realized that just one pile would take him back to Japan tomorrow—even the most determined of men could not help reaching out for it.

Sueko Nakagawa recalled that her dreams of life in the United States were soon contradicted by reality.

In the spring of 1924 I came to the United States accompanied by my husband, in my heart an innocent dream that if we worked hard in the States we could make a lot of money and then return to Japan. We settled down in a Japanese hotel room where his parents were also living. I have a dreary memory of me finally folding my Japanese kimono on the bed and putting it away.

I had to study English...and so I went to night school, escorted to and from by my husband. In the daytime I was to work at Alaska Junk Company where my mother-in-law was working. This was the biggest of the junk companies, dealing in old iron, burlap sacks, used clothes and rags, and old newspapers and magazines. I was put in the old magazine and newspaper section. It was a big wooden building three stories high and the junk was piled up to the ceiling on every floor. The dusty smell filled the building. More than twenty Japanese men and women were working there.... Since there was no heater during the winter, we had to put on so many sweaters that if we happened to tumble over, we couldn't get up without help. Once entering the room, we felt the dust irritate our nose, and during summertime swarms of fleas swarmed up our legs.

Mine Kawamoto, who lived in Florin, California, around 1900, sewed clothing at home. Many Japanese American women helped to support their families through such activities.

Kinji Ushijima (George Shima)

Known as California's "potato king," George Shima rose from poverty to become the first Japanese American millionaire. Yet his financial success did not spare him from prejudice or earn him the right to become a citizen of the United States.

Shima was born Kinji Ushijima in a small town in Japan in 1864. After failing to pass the entrance exam for the University of Tokyo, he emigrated to San Francisco in 1889. Working as a servant, he changed his name and learned to speak English. He took a job as a farm laborer and soon became a labor contractor.

Shima saw that much fertile land in the Sacramento River delta remained unused. Frequent and unpredictable floods had discouraged others from farming on it. Shima and a group of other Issei purchased some land and planted potatoes. By building a system of dikes and using pumps to turn swampland into fields, Shima's enterprise prospered. By 1913, his agribusiness controlled 28,800 acres of land.

Though Shima contributed heavily to charities and paid high taxes, California newspapers printed scare stories about him, warning of a "Japanese takeover." When Shima bought a house in a wealthy Berkeley neighborhood, one headline declared: JAP INVADES FASHIONABLE QUARTERS. He had to agree to build a high fence around his house to appease his neighbors.

In 1909, Shima became president of the Japanese Association of America. In that post he tried to defeat anti-Japanese laws proposed by the state of California and the U.S. Congress. Discouraged by the passage of the California Alien Land Law and the Exclusion Act of 1924, Shima reportedly looked into the possibility of buying farmland in Korea and Mexico. When he died in 1926, the mayor of San Francisco served as a pallbearer at his funeral. It was a small but inadequate tribute to a man who contributed so much to California's agricultural wealth.

WORKING THE FIELDS

Japanese American migrant farm workers were called buranke-katsugi *(blanket carriers) because they carried their bedding with them as they traveled from place to place. Matsato Uyeda, who emigrated by herself to the United States in 1915, recalled her life as a buranke-katsugi on a sugar beet farm in Ogden, Utah.*

My work was thinning and topping. For every acre I finished, I made from $5.50 to $6.00. It was pretty good money for those days. Actually I did one acre and a half per day, so I made $9.00 a day, but it was terribly hard to do day after day. I slept in a tent outside, or in a barn, or in one corner of a storage bin. I spread straw down, put canvas over it, wrapped in a blanket...and slept that way.... I rose at 4:00 in the morning, cooked a simple meal for myself on the stove, and then went out to the fields. As I was not used to this kind of work, my legs and hips became very, very tired, and if I worked too hard in the beginning, leaning over, my face swelled up and in the end I got a nosebleed.

Finishing the morning work, when I tried to eat lunch I could neither sit down on a chair nor bend forward, so, standing, I just poured the food down.... Sharp pains ran up and down my legs and hips so that if I accidentally dropped my chopsticks on the ground, I could scarcely lean over to pick them up.... In mid-summer the temperature went up to from 80 to 100 degrees Fahrenheit. Wearing a straw hat and shirt, or naked from the trousers up, I grappled with this earth.... I wanted to get the agony over with even one day sooner, so I drove myself to work harder—one day more, even one hour more—in order to get over the pains.

In 1903, Seito Saibara bought 300 acres of land near Webster, Texas. He encouraged settlers from Japan to join him with the intention of growing rice that could be exported to Japan. Saibara's son Kiyoaki is fourth from left in this picture.

The Nakamura family packs tomatoes on their farm in Imperial, California, around 1930.

Accustomed to luxury as a child, Michiko Sato Tanaka soon found that life in California as an agricultural laborer was an unending round of hard work, as she later told her daughter.

After the grape pruning season there was nothing to do, so we would go to the asparagus camps in Stockton's Cannery Ranch. We washed and packed the asparagus into boxes for the canneries. Only Japanese did asparagus cutting. We lived in the wash house, lining up boxes and sleeping on top of them. The season lasted for three months from June through August. I remember how hard we worked...wearing boots all day long, stooping in the hot sun....

Pear picking started in Walnut Grove. I said, "Let's go." After pears came peach packing in Marysville. In Marysville the air was so stifling hot that we would arise at three in the morning and quickly pick the peaches before the sun's rays reached their peak. We lived in a vacated schoolhouse and fetched water from a well. Since there was no kitchen, we dug a hole in the earth and placed two metal bars over the hole to cook our food.

Apple packing came next, in Watsonville. I was the cook there. My, I did all the farm work there was to do in America...Papa and I and the children going from place to place. To move was easy. All I had to do was roll up the blankets and say, "Let's go," and soon after, we were gone. Issei—it was the same for all of them. They would bring their children everywhere. "*Sa-a*!" and they would wrap their children in blankets and go.

From Watsonville we moved on to Pismo. We stayed in a house behind a grocery store owned by a *hakujin* (white person). He felt sorry for us living in the camps and he let us live there free. It was the first time I lived in a house since coming to America. In the morning the waves would break, "J-a-h!"

Japanese farm women, probably in California, after changing into their hanahana *outfits.*

near our window. Papa would go fishing and we would dig for clams and cook them over the heat of a lamp. Oh, how delicious!

We worked for Masuoka-san [a Japanese farmer] picking peas. He planted them on the mountain's slope because they grew faster, away from the ocean fog, yet warmed from the gentle salt air. The view from the mountains was breathtaking. We would leave Nesan [her first child] in the car and let her sleep while we picked peas on slopes so steep that you slipped with each step. Already my stomach bulged with child. I worked up to the day Hana was born.

Manyumon Fujita was a sharecropper in Montana in the first decade of the 20th century. As part of his lease contract, he was required to improve a portion of the land. His son Frank remembered how hard his father worked.

My Dad grew dryland beans and sugar beets, mostly. It wasn't easy. I remember him walking through the dirt behind a two-horse plow, wearing "shoes" of canvas bean sacks which were white with blue and red stripes. Almost every spring he had to auction his implements—plow, horses, wagon—to pay his debts. Then he would sign another mortgage at the bank to buy new implements and seed to farm another crop. A good part of the time all we had to eat was fried potatoes and something we called *bottera*—fried batter, like pancakes, stuffed with mashed, sweetened beans. Wherever we lived, it was a two-day wagon trip to town. When Dad took us, he'd head for his favorite saloon and we would go along and fill our bellies with the free lunch that was always avail-

Zenroku and Hinayo Nagai with their son Tadashi, in Rowland, California, in 1914. Berry growing in southern California was pioneered by Japanese immigrants, who owned 80 percent of the industry in the 1920s.

able—cold meats, rye bread, hardboiled eggs, pickles. We were poor, but all the farmers in the area were in the same fix. We were the only Japanese family, and were completely accepted by our neighbors. I didn't know the meaning of discrimination until we quit farming and moved to Seattle.

Sharecroppers were entirely dependent on what the owner of the land would agree to "share." Shoji Takeda described the way his sharecropper father was treated.

Tomiju Takeda, my father, would produce a beautiful crop, but the owner would receive the total compensation from the buyer and without [my father's] knowledge the owner would spend all the money.... One particular incident which was told by my father [was] that the owner had spent my father's share of the income and this led to the owner presenting my father with a Jersey cow as his payment.

In sharecropping families everyone worked on the farms, as Iddy Asada, born in 1928 in California, recalled.

Nattie [her sister] and I would have the task of hoeing the weeds and baby sitting our younger sister Yasuye. But the best thing I remember was the story telling time in the fields. G.T. [Iddy Assada's mother] was subscribing to *Shifu No Tomo* (the Japanese *Ladies Home Journal*) and she would read the serials and tell us the stories while we were working in the fields. When the magazine would arrive the first of each month, we begged her to stay home to read the stories which we would hear while doing our tasks in the fields. We were a poor family but close and a happy family. Tani [Iddy's father] was kind and gentle and he especially loved children.... Many a time he would tell G.T. that he was going fishing and he was going all by himself. He spoke loud enough for us to hear and we would hide in the car until he took off. We would come up from the back and he would act surprised we were there.

Workers harvest cabbages in California in the 1930s. Issei farmers were among the pioneers of the state's huge agricultural industry.

Around 1925, a Japanese American family poses with the latest in farm machinery. It was an early type of tractor.

The Fujimoto family in front of their vegetable stand in El Monte, California, in 1937. The children did their part to make the family business a success.

Yoshimi Yamamoto and Shig Motoki sack potatoes in Eden, Idaho, in 1942. Idaho was outside the designated military zone in which Japanese residents were subject to internment. However, Japanese who fled to other areas from California often faced hostility from Caucasians.

Japanese farmers introduced certain crops to California. Tomiju Takeda, who arrived in the United States in 1907, was working in a hotel kitchen when he first saw celery. His son Shoji retold the story.

On this assignment as a salad cook, there was one vegetable that he was not allowed to handle, which was celery. This caused his curiosity to be aroused. He...asked the chief of the waiters, as to why the vegetable celery was so sacred. The answer was that celery is a very rare commodity, difficult to grow on the Pacific Coast.... Therefore, celery is expensive...rare and many people did not know how to eat this product.

[Tomiju Takeda decided that it might be profitable to grow celery. Two years later, he found a celery field near Palo Alto, California. The Chinese farmer who grew the celery agreed to teach Takeda the proper techniques. In 1914, he rented 10 acres of land in the Santa Clara Valley and planted celery. As his son describes, he faced many hardships.]

One problem was that although the area was ideally suited for the production of celery, flooding occurred.... In the winter of the first year during the harvest season, heavy rains came and flooded the crop half way through harvest. After the flood, motivation still persisted my father to harvest the remainder of the crop by digging out the remaining celery by shovel, one by one, transporting them to the edge of the field, where he washed each head of celery in a stream of artesian water.... Although being very painful and difficult work, he had to do this to survive.

[Eventually, many other Japanese farmers in the valley began to plant celery, with Tomiju Takeda's help. In 1931, they formed a cooperative organization that developed new markets in Chicago and New York for the previously rare vegetable.]

The success of Japanese American farmers created resentment and fears among other California farmers. In 1913 California passed the Alien Land Act, which banned "aliens ineligible for citizenship" from owning land or leasing it for longer than three years. Seven years later, another California law prevented Asian Americans from leasing land or sharecropping. San Jose businessman I. K. Ishimatsu remembered the effect of such legislation.

I don't go so far as to say the alien land laws threatened our livelihood. But if you wanted to lease or own the land for any purpose, you had to use your children's name and if you didn't have your own children, you would have to take a risk and ask someone who was a citizen and hope everything worked out. A set of books had to be kept up for inspection by the state authorities in order to prove that you were an employee working for a wage. This caused an uneasy feeling because I was informed at the time that the punishment for alien land law violation was condemnation of all the subject's property and imprisonment.

Because Japanese American children born in this country were automatically American citizens, farmland could legally be registered in their names. Riichi Satow, who arrived in the United States in 1912, worked for years as a farm laborer before taking a job with a Japanese-language newspaper in San Francisco. Satow described how he moved from that to ownership of a strawberry farm.

Besides my job during the day, I was going to night school to learn English four nights a week. I had three children by then, and my wife was working part-time—embroidery to help make our living.... There were times when she had more income than I did. Both of us really did work hard, and finally my health broke down....

After getting out of the hospital, I came back to Sacramento and started raising strawberries again. We went back to Oak Park, and I leased a ranch. The harvest for that year was just stupendous, and the harvest for the following year was again wonderful.... With the money from the harvest, about three thousand dollars, I bought this place and moved in....

I bought the land under the name of a corporation, because Issei couldn't buy land at that time.

The land registration was then switched from the corporation's into our children's names when they came of age. That's how we handled the matter. I continued growing strawberries and served as president of the Strawberry Growers' Association for some time before the war started.

Workers pick strawberries on the Nagai farm near Rowland, California, in 1914. California's Alien Land Laws were intended to put such farmers out of business. However, many families registered the land in the names of their native-born children, who were legally U.S. citizens.

Anti-Japanese prejudice in California was openly displayed. This float appeared in a Labor Day parade around 1913.

Some California communities required Mexican American and Japanese American children to go to segregated schools. This fifth-grade class was photographed in El Monte, California, around 1940.

PREJUDICE

White laborers, even those who were immigrants themselves, feared that Japanese immigrants would take their jobs. In the 1970s, Shigeru Osawa remembered her experiences with prejudice.

I am a Nisei, born in Seattle in 1891.... In 1905 or 1906... there was a fellow who was connected with a union and used to make speeches against Japanese on the street near a Japanese restaurant. If the union members dined there, he charged them a $5 penalty. Japanese were not permitted to join the union....

In such places as Western-style restaurants run by Japanese, veterans' organizations put their flag at the entrance and huge plug-uglies with sandwich-boards over their shoulders labelled ANTI-JAPS would enter the shops and stand before the customers, impolitely shouting, "Why do you patronize Japs? Get out!" The Japanese owner just had to endure it.

Nisuke Mitsumori emigrated to the United States from Japan in 1905 and found work on a Japanese-language newspaper. He recalled the fear that anti-Japanese prejudice created.

At that time, American feeling toward the Japanese was already bad in general, and we were advised not to walk alone during the day and not to go out at night. It was particularly dangerous after school was over. I never went out at night, and even during the day I tried to avoid the streets where American youngsters might be. I felt very insecure, not economically but physically. I remember those incidents in which young Japanese boys who worked for the paper came back to the office beaten up. It happened frequently. Sometimes we celebrated the fact that we were not hit that day.

California newspapers often whipped up anti-Japanese prejudice by printing fantastic rumors, as Kiyoshi Karl Kawakami explained in 1921.

Somewhere in the Sacramento Valley lived a gentleman who wanted to be a state legislator. He talked a lot about the Japanese menace, and repeatedly stated that the Japanese had leased 10,000,000 acres of land in the upper end of the Sutter Basin. That was great news and the man got all the publicity he wanted. But remember that the Sutter Basin has only 60,000 acres in all. How anyone can lease 10,000,000 acres just in the upper end of it, when the entire basin comprises only 60,000 acres, is beyond the comprehension of a sane man. Yet this wild statement was published in newspapers all over California.... If any intelligent man tried to get the correct statement in the press, it was of no avail because it was not news.

Frank Enseki was born in Hawaii. In 1932, he visited Los Angeles to see the Olympics. He decided to stay but found it difficult to get a job.

I saw a lot of homes going up so I asked if I could get a job as a carpenter.

The man told me that no matter how good I was, he was sorry but he could not give me a job. He said his other men would sit down. They wouldn't work with me.

I asked him why, and he said because I was not white.

I kept looking for work. I would go wherever there was an advertisement for a job, and they would tell me there was no job. Even if the ad was still in the paper. When they saw the color of my face they would say, "I'm sorry. There is no job."

Yoshiko Uchida grew up in Berkeley, California, in the 1930s. In her memoir, Desert Exile, *she described trying to "fit in" with her school classmates.*

As I approached adolescence, I wanted more than anything to be accepted as any other white American.... I saw integration into white American society as the only way to overcome the sense of rejection I had experienced in so many areas of my life....

In high school being different was an even greater hardship than in my younger years. In elementary school one of my teachers had singled out the Japanese American children in class to point to our uniformly high scholastic achievement. (I always worked hard to get A's.) But in high school, we were singled out by our white peers, not for praise, but for total exclusion from their social functions....

Once during my college years, when friends from Los Angeles came to visit, we decided to go dancing, as we occasionally did at the Los Angeles Palladium. But when we went to a ballroom in Oakland, we were turned away by the woman at the box office who simply said, "We don't think you people would like the kind of dancing we do here." That put enough of a damper on our spirits to make us head straight home, too humiliated to go anywhere else to salvage the evening.

Society caused us to feel ashamed of something that should have made us feel proud. Instead of directing anger at the society that excluded and diminished us, such was the climate of the times, and so low our self-esteem that many of us Nisei tried to reject our own Japaneseness and the Japanese ways of our parents....

I would be embarassed when my mother behaved in what seemed to me a non-American way. I would cringe when I was with her as she met a Japanese friend on the street and began a series of bows, speaking all the while in Japanese.

"Come on, Mama," I would interrupt, tugging at her sleeve. "Let's go," I would urge, trying to terminate the long exchange of amenities. I felt disgraced in public.

These are some 1905 headlines from the San Francisco Chronicle, *probably the most influential newspaper on the West Coast at the time:*

THE JAPANESE INVASION, THE PROBLEM OF THE HOUR

JAPANESE A MENACE TO AMERICAN WOMEN

BROWN MEN AN EVIL IN THE PUBLIC SCHOOLS

BROWN ARTISANS STEAL BRAINS OF WHITES

CRIME AND POVERTY GO HAND IN HAND WITH ASIATIC LABOR

Japanese Americans who could afford to move into middle-class neighborhoods sometimes found their homes vandalized. The prejudice was worst in California, which had a larger number of Issei than any other state—though the percentage of Japanese Americans was only about 1 percent before World War II.

71

The Sakatani family of El Monte, California, in 1934.

CHAPTER FIVE

PUTTING DOWN ROOTS

n the 1870s, the first Japanese students and job seekers settled in San Francisco, where the Japanese government maintained a consulate. After 1906, when much of San Francisco was devastated by earthquake and fire, many Japanese residents moved south to Los Angeles. That city's Little Tokyo became the largest Japanese American community on the mainland. Meanwhile, Japanese communities also sprang up in such cities as Sacramento, Fresno, Portland, Seattle, Tacoma, and Salt Lake City, as well as the Hawaiian cities of Honolulu and Hilo.

Most of these early communities began around immigrant boardinghouses. Nearby stores sold Japanese food such as tofu, noodles, fish cakes, and soy sauce. Issei city dwellers resumed their former occupations—as tailors, pottery makers, carpenters, and blacksmiths, for example. Bathhouses, where Japanese could enjoy a hot communal pool as they had at home, became part of the growing communities. Women, too, went into business, primarily as laundresses and midwives.

With the arrival of significant numbers of women after 1908, family life became more apparent in Japanese American communities. The Issei family resembled its counterpart in Japan. Its relationships were determined by the ideal of *on*, or sense of obligation. *Otoosan*, the father, was the absolute head of the household; his decisions were followed without hesitation. He was served first at mealtimes and received the best portions.

Children, especially sons, were regarded as the treasures of the family. The first son was particularly important, for he was responsible for carrying on the family name. It was his obligation to care for his parents in their old age, and after their deaths he was expected to care for their graves and make the required prayers at the family shrine.

Okaa-san, the mother, was responsible for the good order of the household. She took charge of the training of the children, careful to instill in them the traditional Japanese values. Typically, *okaa-san* put her children's welfare above her own. When bathwater was drawn, the father used it first, followed by the male children from oldest to youngest, then the daughters, and finally *okaa-san*.

Most of the Japanese American immigrants were Buddhists. Japanese in Hawaii founded the islands' first Buddhist temple in 1894; five years later one was built in San Francisco. Buddhist priests held a place of great respect in the Japanese American communities. They carried out the important rituals of birth, marriage, and death, as well as festivals like *Obon*, in which the spirits of the dead are welcomed back to earth for a night. Buddhist priests also read and wrote letters for the illiterate, mediated disputes, and formed community organizations such as the Young Men's Buddhist Association.

Virtually all Japanese Americans also followed the traditions of Shinto, the Japanese belief in nature-spirits. A public Shinto shrine, the Yamato Jinja, was built on the island of Hawaii in 1898. Each Japanese household usually had its own small Shinto shrine, where offerings of fruit and flowers were regularly placed to honor family ancestors.

Christian missionaries, however, did make converts among Japanese Americans. The very first organization founded by Japanese Americans was the Fukuinkai, or Gospel Society, started in 1877 in San Francisco. In 1894 the Reverend Takie Okumura arrived in Hawaii. Born in Japan, he had been ordained a Protestant minister there. He became a leading member of the Japanese Hawaiian community, founding a boarding school where he introduced the sport of baseball.

For some Issei and Nisei, becoming a Christian was part of the process of becoming American. By most estimates, a majority of Japanese Americans both in Hawaii and the mainland belong to some

Christian denomination today.

Most Nisei children attended public schools, and a sizable number enrolled in American colleges. Yet they too were held back by bigotry and prejudice. Before the end of World War II, college-educated Nisei were forced into farming, small businesses, and jobs as servants or gardeners. Even those who became doctors and lawyers could only practice in the "Little Tokyos" of western cities.

To keep alive the sense of tradition in their children, Japanese Americans founded schools where the Nisei learned Japanese customs and language. Schools also taught Japan's traditional sports of judo, *sumo* wrestling, and *kendo*, or wooden-sword fighting. The motivation behind these sports was to learn self-control and discipline. Some Nisei were sent back to Japan for education; they were known as *Kibei*.

Like all immigrant groups, the Issei founded numerous protective and mutual aid associations. These groups represented Japanese Americans in civic affairs, offered aid to those in need, and provided interpreters to help people deal with local government officials. *Kenjinkai*—associations of people who came from a particular prefecture in Japan—organized social affairs, such as annual picnics that were festive occasions in most Japanese American communities.

The first national organization, the Japanese Association of America (JAA), was founded in San Francisco in 1908 to fight the discriminatory laws of western states. The JAA acquired consider-able power because the Japanese government authorized it to issue travel visas for Issei to visit Japan and certificates that enabled picture brides to emigrate.

The JAA's close ties to the Japanese government embarrassed some Nisei, who felt that it encouraged white Americans' suspicions of "dual loyalty." In 1930, Nisei from California, Washington, and Oregon organized the first national convention of the Japanese American Citizens League (JACL). As the JACL grew—mostly in the Pacific

Before World War II, Japanese American communities thrived in many of the large cities on the Pacific coast. Here, the Japanese Chamber of Commerce of Portland, Oregon, has decorated a float for a parade in the 1930s.

Coast states—its members stressed their loyalty to the country of their birth.

The Nisei faced another dilemma during the 1930s, when the Japanese government invaded Chinese territory. This policy created tensions between Japan and the United States, which supported the Chinese government. The United States banned the export of certain kinds of war-related materials to Japan.

On December 7, 1941, while Japanese diplomats were in Washington, D.C., to discuss differences between the two nations, Japanese planes bombed the U.S. naval base at Pearl Harbor, Hawaii. The following day, President Franklin D. Roosevelt asked Congress to declare war on Japan.

The outbreak of World War II marked the beginning of a nightmare for Japanese Americans. Hundreds of them were immediately arrested by agents of the Federal Bureau of Investigation. Most were Issei community leaders whose names had been placed on a list of potential "enemy aliens." For the next two months, other Japanese Americans faced taunts and humiliation.

Newspapers fanned the war fever, which made anyone with a Japanese face an enemy. Rumors spread that Japan was planning an attack on the mainland United States, and all Japanese Americans were suspected of being saboteurs who would assist this invasion (which never occurred).

Before the war began, President Roosevelt had received the Munson Report—a secret study that indicated the great majority of the Japanese Americans were loyal to the United States, and would remain so in case of war with Japan. Nevertheless, on February 19, 1942, Roosevelt issued Executive Order No. 9066. It authorized the War Department to "prescribe military areas...from which any or all persons may be excluded."

Less than a month later, General John L. DeWitt created two such military areas, which included all of California, Washington, and Oregon as well as southern Arizona. The army then began to move

Japanese Americans out of these areas on the grounds that they were threats to American security.

Japanese Americans facing forced removal were told they could bring only what they could carry. They sold their homes and businesses for whatever they could get; entire communities were wiped out in only a few months' time. At first they were taken to assembly centers, from which they were assigned to "relocation camps," which were American-style concentration camps. By September 1942, tens of thousands of Japanese Americans had been interned in 10 camps in isolated areas.

Some Hawaiian Japanese were sent to mainland camps, and in 1943, a detention camp was established on the island of Oahu. But because Japanese farmers were so important to the economy of the islands, most Hawaiian Japanese were spared internship.

The internees in the camps did their best to form a community life, for no one knew how long the war would last. They elected governing councils, established schools, and started newspapers. Crops were planted to give the internees useful work. But no matter how "normal" life became, nothing could conceal the fact that the camps were surrounded by barbed-wire fences and guarded by soldiers. When a group of residents at the Manzanar camp in California gathered to protest the arrest of three men, military police fired into the crowd. Two were killed, and at least 10 more injured. Such incidents took place at other camps as well.

Japanese Americans in the camps were given a "loyalty" questionnaire to determine whether their sympathies lay with the United States or Japan. One question was, "Will you swear unqualified allegiance to the United States of America and forswear any form of allegiance or obedience to

After the outbreak of World War II, Japanese Americans in the western states were sent to American-style concentration camps. The Taniguchi family poses at the Poston, Arizona, camp in 1943. Months later, Kazuto Taniguchi, top row at left, joined the all-Nisei 442nd Regimental Combat Team.

the Japanese emperor?" This was particularly insulting to Nisei, who were U.S. citizens and had never sworn allegiance to the emperor. Few of their parents had either unless they had served in the Japanese military before emigrating.

Yet anyone who protested the forced removal or failed the loyalty examination was classified as disloyal. One of the camps, at Tule Lake in northern California, was designated a "segregation center" for those regarded as particularly dangerous.

Eventually, some internees who "proved" their loyalty were permitted to leave. However, they were not allowed to return to their former homes, which were in areas now designated as military zones. Some "voluntarily" resettled in other parts of the United States.

Another question asked to test a person's loyalty was, "Are you willing to serve in the armed forces of the United States on combat duty?" Indeed, many Nisei volunteered for the U.S. armed forces. Some became translators with U.S. troops in the Pacific and Asia; the majority served in the all-Nisei 442nd Regimental Combat Team, which was sent to fight in Europe. The men of the 442nd distinguished themselves for bravery. It was the most decorated unit of its size in U.S. military history.

Out of a total mainland population of less than 150,000, about 120,000 Japanese Americans were sent to the concentration camps. Two-thirds of them were Nisei—native-born citizens who were stripped of their rights without accusation or trial. It was the most massive violation of civil rights in U.S. history.

Some Nisei resisted the relocation orders and were sent to prison. A few appealed their convictions to higher courts. In December 1944, the U.S. Supreme Court issued a ruling in the case of *Korematsu* v. *United States*. By a 6-to-3 vote, the Court declared that the relocation orders were legal. Justice Frank Murphy wrote a stirring dissent: "This exclusion of 'all people of Japanese ancestry, both alien and non-alien'...goes over 'the very brink of constitutional power' and falls into the ugly abyss of racism."

The Asahi baseball team in Treasure Valley, Oregon, in the 1930s. Japanese Americans were particularly fond of this American sport. There were organized teams in Hawaii as early as the 19th century.

A street scene from the Little Tokyo section of Los Angeles in the 1930s. The corner of East First and San Pedro Streets, the site of the Miyako Hotel, was known as the crossroads of Japanese America.

COMMUNITY LIFE

In San Francisco, early Japanese immigrants rented houses in the area around 3rd and 7th Streets, paying $10 to $15 a month. Decades later, Washizu Bunzo described what the neighborhood was like in the 1890s.

This entire area was a San Francisco slum.... All the houses were so small and dirty that one could not use them to store things now....

When I arrived in America, we didn't need addresses to visit Japanese homes. As long as we were told of such-and-such intersecting streets, we always found the houses. We had only to look for basements with sooty curtains to find them. There we invariably found Japanese living in cave-like dwellings....

Corresponding to these dwellings, the kitchens were filthy and disorderly to the extreme. There were no stoves as the boardinghouses had. All cooking was done on one or two-burner oil stoves. We brewed coffee, toasted bread, and grilled smoked salmon on these oil stoves. Thick, black smoke darkened the rooms, and we were oblivious to the odor which assailed our nostrils.

Japantowns grew up around labor camps where the Japanese workers lived in barracks. Eventually, boardinghouses opened to cater to the Japanese. Masuo Akizuki recalled life in a San Jose, California, boardinghouse in the early years of the 20th century.

When I came to San Jose the day after my arrival, everybody was working in the countryside. The boarding houses in San Jose Japantown found jobs for us. They brought us by horse carriage to the place to work, and we each were given one blanket. Our living conditions were miserable at that time. We slept next to a horse stable on our blankets and some straw. It was so miserable Sansei [third-generation Japanese Americans] may not be able to believe it. When we finished the work, we went back to the boarding house and rested there until the next job came around.

By the 1930s, Los Angeles had the largest concentration of Japanese Americans. Mary Oyama Mittwer described what she called "Li'l Tokyo."

Li'l Tokyo in Los Angeles was a busy, buzzing little place as the center of California's Southland for *Issei* and their *Nisei* offspring. The *Nisei* were already beginning to hold big-time dances with full orchestra, renting ballrooms with glass floors and fancy settings.... *Nisei* social life also centered around the churches such as the Union Church (originally

Congregational) in Li'l Tokyo, in uptown West-side's Japanese Methodist Church...and St. Mary's Episcopal Church.

The Japanese community's shopping and trading, especially for the *Issei*, centered around the hub of the East First and San Pedro intersection. The landmark Miyako Hotel, the Asia Company dry goods store, the theater where Japanese movies were shown, restaurants and cafes, the professional offices, drew the Japanese populace from the rest of the city and the surrounding rural areas.

City kids used to say they could tell country *Nisei* who came to town "because they wear white hats and white shoes." Some of the latter, as well as the locals, would stop at Tomio's department store, dine at the Kawafuku, while bachelor fieldhands on weekends would drink in small cafes or shoot a round in the local pool halls....

As a whole, *Nisei* in Los Angeles lived in fairly new, better and more comfortable homes than did their counterparts in Northern California. Their homes were *hakujin* (white people) style, with trees, lawns and ample back yards rather than being in old, decrepit buildings in the shabby part of town as in other Japanese centers. This was because in the 1930's Los Angeles was still a wide-spaced, green-lawn town, horizontal, and with lots of room for expansion. The Japanese also were beginning to acquire cars, one to a family, to meet the transportation needs of the sprawling city.... To the *Issei*, it seemed the *Nisei* were always running around. They grumbled, "One o'clock, two o'clock—never come home. Too much-i dan-su, dan-su." But somehow the *Nisei* survived their rounds of sports events, dances, conventions and other activities without becoming delinquents.

Toward the later 1930's the Los Angeles *Issei* and *Nisei* community inaugurated the annual Nisei Week Festival highlighted by a queen contest, baby show, and Japanese folk dances in the streets. The non-Japanese public came to see, buy and dine in Li'l Tokyo, and Japanese businessmen smiled happily. Life was fairly comfortable in our comparatively insulated world which we at that time did not recognize as being an ethnic ghetto in today's connotation of the expression.

In California, Japanese Americans lived in a virtually segregated society. Kyoko Oshima Takayanagi, who was born in Oakland, California, in 1924, remembered how she became aware of this situation.

We played with neighborhood kids, so there was a mixed group. But as we got older, it was a little different. We were very friendly with them at school, but our social life was separate. I remember in high school there was a Hi-Y—it's like a teenage senior-high club. It was segregated, all Japanese-American, *Nisei....* There was a *Nisei* segregated basketball league and baseball league, and there was a girl's basketball league. They'd have different segregated dances.

Little Tokyos within American West Coast cities were, as the name implies, very much like towns in Japan. Izo Kojima recalled the Japanese section of Seattle at the time of his arrival in 1918:

In Japanese town around Jackson and Main [were] cafes, restaurants, Chinese restaurants, noodle shops, sushi shops, a condiments store, a *tofu* store, groceries, drug stores, a pool hall, ten-cent stores.... One couldn't believe he was abroad, and one didn't even need to speak English.

Two women chat on River Street in Honolulu around 1930. By 1930, nearly half the retail businesses in Hawaii were owned by Japanese Americans.

Just as Irish immigrants felt kinship to those who were born in the same county in Ireland, Japanese Americans gathered with others from the same prefecture, or ken. Akemi Kikumura, a modern Japanese American scholar, quoted "an old-timer who had settled in Seattle":

There was a tendency toward the concentration of people from the same prefectures in Japan at the same places and in the same lines of work. For example, the barbers in Seattle, at least in the old days, all tended to be people from Yamaguchi-ken.... Then again, in the restaurant business, the majority of them were Ehime-ken.... Homes like those of Mr. I. were places where young men congregated who were eager to learn things and discuss them, and in the course of their association, they learned such trades as their friends knew.

The Yodogawa sushi shop in Honolulu. Sushi is a small roll of cold cooked rice and vinegar wrapped in seaweed, like those seen on the shop's banner. Sushi filling may also include egg, vegetables, or fish. Raw fish cut into small pieces and served by itself is called sashimi.

In the tightly knit Japanese American communities, young Nisei faced social pressure to behave in a "proper" manner, as Hiroshi Asai, who grew up in Cortez, California, described.

You've got to be careful how you act. You've got to face your community, whereas if you're not that tied down, and if you do something bad you move and in the next place you've got a fresh start, you've got another chance. But over here [laughing], somebody will remember 50 years [later] if you've done something, he'll still remember. So you've got that pressure on you.

In Hawaii, Japanese American communities grew up on the sugarcane plantations. Baishiro Tamashiro, who went to Hawaii from Okinawa in 1906, told interviewer Michiko Kodama in 1980 about the extensive social life that had existed on the plantations.

There were plantations located in different areas. At the nine plantations there were Okinawan clubs; these clubs joined together and formed the *Rengo-Kai*. That started in 1922 or 1923. The president was Mr. Kina. I was vice president. The organization was very successful. It was quite popular, that club. At the time there were about 2,000 Okinawans living on Kauai and over 1,000 were members.... We had *ji no tenrankai* (calligraphy exhibition) and *onago no shugei no tenrankai* (women's embroidery exhibition). Also once a month we had various books (*zasshi*) on display...it was very successful. New Year's parties were very popular. We had one in Kapaa, then one in Koloa, Makaweli, Kekaha...the place changed every year. They used to give lots of speeches at these things. As many as 20 people would give speeches. We also had *bon* dances. Around 1926, to raise money we held a sword dance show (*kenbu* show) and made about $1000.

On Boys' Day (May 5) and the corresponding Girls' Day (March 3), Japanese children are honored by their families and communities. Here, Boys' Day carp banners (koinobori) decorate a street in Hawaii in 1923. The carp symbolize strength.

Usaburo Katamoto, born in Nakajima, Japan, in 1896, emigrated to Hawaii as a child. In 1915, the Katamoto family returned to Japan, where Usaburo was married. He went back to Hawaii with this bride in 1920. They moved into a rented house in Kakaako, Honolulu. In 1978, two years before his death, Katamoto told interviewers about his life in Kakaako.

The owner of the house made it for two family to live. My wife and I had three rooms—kitchen-dining room, living room and a very small bedroom. At first, we had only kerosene lamp, but later on we had electric light. We had to buy a bed because I did very hard work and couldn't get used to sleeping on the floor. The bed just fit in the bedroom. Toilet was inside the house, because we had sewer system in the area. And we took showers in a semi-public place. We bought all our supplies and groceries from the Fujikawas who had the bathhouse, so we didn't pay anything for the use of their facilities....

At that time, in Kakaako, there were many places, or camps, like ours. On Punchbowl Street there was two blocks like that, too. Each block had about twenty families. And they had one grocery store which would supply the whole area. All kind of different merchants would supply the families. And, everything's on credit those days 'cause that's the only way you can do business. There's no such thing as cash and carry because people, especially Japanese immigrants, didn't have enough cash. And the storekeepers around our area were usually Japanese and some Chinese. You remember, there was quite few Japanese in Kakaako, that is, our area.

Jeanne Wakatsuki spent the first six years of her life in Ocean Park, California, where her family was the only Japanese one. When the family moved to Terminal Island, where 500 Japanese families lived, it was a shock.

In those days, [Terminal Island] was a company town, a ghetto owned and controlled by the canneries. The men went after fish, and whenever the boats came back—day or night—the women would be called to process the catch while it was fresh. One in the afternoon or four in the morning, it made no difference. My mother had to go to work right after we moved there. I can still hear the whistle—two toots for French's, three for Van Camp's—and she and Chizu would be out of bed in the middle of the night, heading for the cannery.

The house we lived in was nothing more than a shack, a barracks with single plank walls and rough wooden floors, like the cheapest kind of migrant workers' housing. The people around us were hardworking, boisterous, a little proud of their nickname, *yo-go-re*, which meant literally uncouth one, or roughneck.... They not only spoke Japanese exclusively, they spoke a dialect peculiar to Kyushu, where their families had come from in Japan, a rough, fisherman's language, full of oaths and insults.... They would swagger and pick on outsiders and persecute anyone who didn't speak as they did. That was

The Japanese American Citizens League sponsored both political and social events. Mary Oyama Mittwer, a member of the league in the 1930s, wrote:

Between wienie bakes and the beaches and dances, *Nisei* would gather at church and JACL meetings to ponder ways of getting out the *Nisei* vote, planning ways of putting up Japanese American candidates for political offices, mixing more into the larger American community, talking about the future of Japanese churches and citizenship for the *Issei*.

Japanese American children on the running board of a 1920s car. The Issei, who were ineligible for citizenship, placed their hopes for success in their children, who were citizens by birth.

Families and neighbors join together for mochitsuki—*preparing rice cakes for the New Year's celebration. The cakes are made from a special type of rice that is pounded with wooden mallets after being cooked.*

The Japanese American Citizens League was founded in 1930 by delegates from California, Washington, Oregon, and Hawaii. Today, it is still the leading national organization of Japanese Americans.

what made my own time there so hateful. I had never spoken anything but English, and the other kids in the second grade despised me for it.

The Japanese hall was the social and cultural center of Japanese American communities. There, people enjoyed traditional plays and music, practiced martial arts, and socialized. A Nisei woman who lived in Del Rey, California, remembered the movies that were shown in the hall.

There was a Japanese bachelor, he fooled around with a camera and movies, he was kind'a hep on that kind of stuff. He ran the projection machine.

Later on a traveling man, go town to town and show these *samurai* movies [from Japan] on weekends.... Folks sponsor the movie too, sort of like a benefit.

Everybody gave donation to see the movie and they write it all on a piece of paper, big paper with our name and how much we donate in Japanese. [The person writing down the amounts of the donations] would double it those days, to make the others dish out more. If you donate ten dollars they'd put up twenty, that's what everybody would do....

The Hall was packed, it was always a full house. The whole family would go, babies and all. It was their only outlet, it was a big to do.

Japanese American clubs and associations often sponsored exhibitions of Japanese sports, such as sumo wrestling or kendo (wooden-sword fighting). Frank M. Tomori recalled the sports scene in Portland, Oregon, around 1910.

The Japanese Association in Portland often held sumo matches in the Armory Hall or in a large garage.... At such an event many Japanese gathered, coming from various towns and villages.... The sumo wrestlers were amateurs from various places. I myself played in the matches among top-ranked wrestlers.... Although we didn't wear the traditional hairdo, we wore ornamental aprons presented by our patrons, and the referee was fully dressed in the traditional ceremonial style. The "Sumo Jinku" (a lively song) was sung, and a display of wrestlers in the ring followed.

In summer, Japanese American clubs and schools sponsored picnics. In her book Nisei Daughter, *Monica Sone recalled one such affair from her girlhood in Seattle.*

Every Japanese in the community turned out and all parents bought new clothes for their children. There was a terrific run on children's tennis shoes in the Japanese shoe stores, for the foot races were the most important event of the picnic....

Hundreds of Japanese swarmed over the beautiful, sprawling green lawn of the picnic ground. It was a grand feeling to be away from the city heat and traffic. Here there was nothing more confining than the graceful poplars, the cool breeze from

Puget Sound and the wide expanse of blue sky....

We [the children] chewed our nails, waiting our turn and wondering what our race would be this year. In the past, the girls in my class had run trying to balance a small bouncy rubber ball on a wooden spoon. We had tried to pick slick lima beans from the ground, one by one, with wooden chopsticks....

The suspense grew more intense as we moved closer to the starting line. When the girls in front of us dashed off on their race, it was our turn to receive instructions. The instructor was Mr. Oshashi, sporty in white duck trousers, white shirt and green-visored cap.... With pounding hearts and clammy cold hands, we listened to him as if we were getting instructions for a final examination.

"This is a 'matching' race! You will find envelopes on the ground, containing cards with *kanji* [symbols]. You must match them with cards lying [elsewhere on the ground]."

When Mr. Ohashi blew the "go" whistle, I leaped forward like a frightened rabbit. I sped halfway around the track and picked up an envelope [with five *kanji*].... I scurried around, bumping into girls, looking for the matching [cards]. By a miracle I was the second person to complete the task and I ran toward the finish line, my heart beating with joy. Then suddenly my toe caught in the grass and I fell flat on my face. The spectators groaned in sympathy. I finished an ignoble number 12 with two raw, bleeding knees....

[After lunch] the crowed moved...to watch the local boys play off their annual baseball tournament. The scene was gay and colorful with bobbing, twirling parasols, bright fans and handkerchiefs excitedly fluttering up breezes. Throwing aside all Japanese restraint, the Issei men shed their hats and dignity and yelled themselves hoarse for their sons and favorite team.... Even the reticent Japanese women shrieked involuntarily as they saw a boy slide for base and disappear in a cloud of dust with the baseman diving right on top of him.

The Omiya family and their store in South Park, California, around 1915.

Clubs in Japanese American communities kept alive the traditions of the old country. Here, a meeting of the Tea Ceremony and Flower Arrangement Club of El Centro, California, around 1930. The tea ceremony originated among Zen Buddhist monks, who thought that its formally polite ritual tended to clear the mind.

FAMILY

The Omishi family of Salem, Oregon, was photographed in 1910.

The family was the center of Japanese American life, with the father firmly entrenched as its head. Akemi Kikumura, a Nisei, described her father's role in her family.

From his wife and children, he expected and demanded steadfast discipline. His primary concern within the household was to maintain family order and unity and the way he chose to do that was by emphasizing traditional patterns: respect and unquestioned obedience to parents and to elder siblings was the rule that governed the household members. Papa would discipline the children, and even instruct Mama on how to prepare various Japanese foods, how to wear a kimono, how to walk like a refined lady, or how to iron a shirt. The daughters recalled that "Everything we heard, knew, felt, or dreamed of came from within the household." Papa forbade his daughters to date, or to engage in any social activity that did not include the family. Even choice of marriage partners was up to his discretion. He lectured each night during dinner on every subject imaginable while everyone listened in silence. Most of the lectures pertained to some aspect of Japanese traditions, values, or etiquette.

A Los Angeles family celebrates Christmas in the 1930s. Many Japanese Americans took up the customs of their adopted land; some had already converted to Christianity before leaving Japan.

Yoshiko Uchida, who grew up in Berkeley, California, in the 1930s, lovingly described her parents in her book Desert Exile.

My father was indeed a businessman in every sense. He was practical and pragmatic, and possessed tremendous energy, enthusiasm, and a joyful eagerness to accomplish successfully any endeavor he undertook. He did everything quickly, from working, to eating, to walking. He was always in a hurry to get wherever he was going and, once there, left promptly when his mission was accomplished. My mother, on the other hand, was exactly the opposite, and I think she found it difficult to feel constantly rushed by Papa. Being a Japanese woman, however, she behaved as a Japanese wife, and adjusted even to having Papa stride several paces ahead of her, not from arrogance, but from impatience. For many years she sat in the back seat of the car, too self-conscious to take the seat up in front beside my father. It is possible, however, she felt safer there, for Papa was a terrible driver, and caused Mama to clutch frequently at whoever sat next to her, calling out, "Be careful, Papa San! Be careful!"

Tamemasu and Yetsu Kamiya with their children and another relative, around 1919. They were members of the Florida Yamato Colony, a farming co-operative. (Yamato is another name for Japan.) Such colonies were also founded in California and Texas during the early 20th century.

Both sons and daughters of Issei expected that their parents would arrange for them marriages to suitable partners. A family would usually employ a baishakunin, *or go-between, to negotiate the details of the marriage with the other family. Michiko Sato Tanaka described the wedding of her daughter Chieko to a man named Jim. (She calls him "Jim-san," using the suffix that is a term of respect.)*

Their wedding was a very proper one. We traveled to Fresno with Nishimoto-san, our *baishakunin*, and our relatives. Jim-san's relatives were dressed in their finest clothes for the occasion. An elaborate spread of food awaited us and artfully packed in boxes for each guest to take home were fish, shrimp, *yokan* (sweet bean jelly), fish cakes, and a cooked vegetable and meat dish. The wedding ceremony was at the Buddhist temple, followed by a reception at a Chinese restaurant.

Before the wedding bonds are tied, each family's *baishakunin* makes visits to the other's family to discuss the wedding plans. The groom's *baishakunin* presents the bride with the *yuino* [betrothal gift money], half of which she spends on making preparations for the wedding and the other half of which she brings to her husband's house after their marriage. In Japanese tradition the groom pays for everything, but for that reason the bride must bring her own quilts, a dresser, and various items for her own personal needs. There are some who say, just bring enough to stuff in a cloth wrapper....

Arranged marriages mediated by a *baishakunin* are good. The mediation binds the marriage well. If there is trouble in the marriage, the *baishakunin* tries to iron out the problems. The married couple is not free to do as they please, and when *tanin* (nonrelatives) intervene and give their judgment in a dispute, it holds great weight.

Henry Katsuji and Takako Hashitani in Emmett, Idaho, in 1912.

The Takasumi family assembles for a group photo in Oregon in the early 1930s. The Japanese extended family offered a crucial support system, and children were raised in an atmosphere of love, learning respect for their elders through example.

Kazuo and Isino Inukai in their apartment in Dee, Oregon, in 1917. They have acquired a number of possessions, including a gramophone, an early type of phonograph.

Japanese American families always gathered to celebrate holidays together. Yoshiko Uchida described her family's joyful celebration of the Japanese New Year in the 1930s.

Each New Year's we took the Southern Pacific overnight sleeper [railroad car with beds] to Los Angeles to spend the holiday with my paternal grandmother who lived with my aunt, uncle, and six cousins. Although there were five adults and eight children crammed into a small bungalow with only one bathroom, my cousins obligingly doubled up and we somehow managed and had great times together....

New Year's was a special time in the early Issei households, for in Japan it is considered a time of renewal and new beginnings. Houses were cleaned, outstanding bills were paid before year's end, and a vast fresh start made in life. It was a time of joyous celebration and vast amounts of special holiday dishes were prepared.

We began our New Year's meal in Los Angeles with bowls of hot broth and toasted rice cakes. In the center of the long table was a long broiled lobster, bright and colorful, symbolizing long life. There were tiered lacquer boxes filled with shredded *daikon* and sesame seed salad, sweetened black beans and lima beans (for good health), knots of seaweed (which I loved), and herring roe (which I could have done without). There were great platters filled with chicken, bamboo shoots, carrots, burdock, taro and lotus root, and hardboiled eggs cut into fancy shapes. Most of the dishes had special symbolism and were prepared over several days.

There was a strong sense of family at these three-generational gatherings and to commemorate the occasion we often had a two-family portrait taken.

The furo, *or communal bath, was a feature of many Japanese American households, as Yoichi Norman Kishi, who grew up in Terry, Texas, recalled.*

Every family had a Japanese bath to relax their muscles. Our bath was in a bathhouse about ten feet away from our house. It was a wooden tub with a metal bottom. You would wash with soap and water and rinse off before you got in the tub. Then you stepped into the tub and sat down on a wooden platform. The water came up to your neck. It was very hot. There was a brick oven underneath the tub. We built a fire in the oven to heat the water.

When I was young, it was my duty to prepare the bath for the family. Every day after I got home from school, I built the fire. I knew just how many sticks of wood to put on the fire. It took ten sticks to make the fire hot enough.

It wasn't a chore I dreaded. I didn't have to watch the fire all the time. I could go off and play. Once in a while the fire would go out, and I would get a scolding.

Elderly members of the family, male or female, command the greatest respect. In Japanese tradition, the 88th birthday is a special one. Rose Tashiro Mitamura described the one held for her mother, who had spent 55 years farming in New Mexico.

When Mother had her 88th birthday, her six children, including myself, gave her a big celebration. Relatives came from Colorado, California, all over. Some of our relatives came from Japan. In Japan, a person's 88th birthday has special significance. It is a custom dating back to the ages when it was very rare for a person to live to be that old. It was believed that at 88 a person is reborn again and the celebration hinges on the long life of the turtle and the crane. All the families together made a thousand and one cranes. The cranes are made out of paper. The art work is called "Origami"—which means folded paper. On her birthday the cranes were all strung together and it was a beautiful thing. The saying in Japan is, "A turtle can live a hundred years but the crane lives a thousand." It symbolizes long life. Mother had a long and eventful life, but she died in 1979 a few months after her 88th birthday. At that time she had 22 grandchildren and two great-grandchildren. Her Buddhist name, Shaku Ni Jisho, is shown on her "In Memory of" card as well as her given name, Tatsue Tashiro.

In this wedding portrait taken in Hawaii around 1915, the bride is dressed in traditional Japanese wedding garments while her husband wears an American-style suit.

Fufaichi and Midori Koda and their children William and George in Kent, Washington, in 1924. Like many other Americans of that prosperous decade, Japanese Americans proudly purchased their first automobile.

Robert and John Fuyuume in 1928 in Los Angeles. During World War II, they and their relatives went to Seabrook, New Jersey, where a food-processing business hired Japanese Americans forced out of their homes on the West Coast. Today John Fuyuume is the project director of the Seabrook Educational and Cultural Center.

Dr. Alice Murata was born in Los Angeles in 1940. Today, she is an education professor at Northeastern Illinois University in Chicago. She remembers her father as an eternal optimist who placed importance on learning through repetition.

Our family, like other Japanese American families, participated in daily routines where values were taught by repetitive "doing." Little attention was placed on emotions. For example, the imporance of patriotism. When I started kindergarten at five years old I related to my father that I couldn't understand why we started each school day by pledging the flag and singing, "My Country 'Tis of Thee." I had difficulty remembering all those words. He said it was to become patriotic, and asked if I was. My response was, "I don't know, what's patriotic?" He replied, "It is when you are proud to be an American and are willing to do anything for your country, even die." When I didn't say anything, he reassured me with, "It's all right, just keep pledging and you will become patriotic." By habitually repeating tasks that were considered developmentally proper, my father thought that appropriate feelings could be learned. For this reason he paid attention to what I was doing.

Nisei tended to adopt American social customs more readily than the first generation of immigrants. Gatherings like this one, in which young men and women met to dance and socialize, were a departure from the traditions of their Issei parents.

Amy Uno Ishii recalled the values of her Issei parents, who were "childhood sweethearts" in Japan. Both were Christians, which strengthened their bond.

When my father came to America [in 1906] to make this his new home, my mother expressed a desire to come. If it was possible for her to come later and marry him...she would like it that way....

[In the United States, he found a job as a foreman for a railroad track gang.]

Around that time, many of the men who were working on the railroad were saving their money and sending for what was called "picture brides" to come from Japan. My mother was not one of these. This is one thing my parents were very, very happy and proud of....

The happiness of my parents was proved to us many times. Although we didn't have material things to make us happy when we were growing up, like a lot of other people who were able to have the most modern up-to-date things, my mother always said: "We don't have a lot of money and we don't have the material things other people have, but I know one thing—we are very rich in happiness and contentment because we have our children. Later on, the years will be nothing but happiness and contentment for us; the material things will come later. God will take care of things."

Rakurai Ikeda (at right) with his sons, daughter-in-law, and newborn grandson.

The family of Shintaro Takamiya built a torii gate in Los Angeles to celebrate his 61st birthday. In Japanese tradition, that birthday marks the rebirth of a person and the start of his or her second childhood.

Children in a public school in San Francisco pledge allegiance to the flag in 1942. Within months, the Japanese American children were sent to detention camps along with their parents and other relatives of Japanese descent.

SCHOOL

Japanese parents, especially the Issei, who could never become citizens, placed their hopes in their children. They believed that education would enable their children to leave the drudgery of plantation work. The daughter of a plantation worker in Hawaii recalled how her father instilled in her a belief in the importance of education.

Father made up his mind to send his children to school so far as he possibly could. Yet he had no idea of forcing us. Instead he employed different methods which made us want to go to school. We were made to work in the cane fields at a very early age.... After a day's work in the fields dad used to ask "Are you tired? Would you want to work in the fields when you are old enough to leave school?"... My father did everything in his power to make us realize that going to school would be to our advantage.

Mary Nagao was born in 1920 in San Bernardino, California, the only child of immigrant parents. Her father was a vegetable farmer and also worked as a cook. She grew up in many places in southern California. She remembered that even though the public schools were integrated, that did not guarantee equal treatment for all.

When I went to school there was something like a gentlemen's agreement. You kind of accepted it because it was done that way. As you grow up, of course, you realize that it isn't that way at all.

For instance, the Mexican and Japanese children were usually seated at the back of the classroom. If the new textbooks ran out as they were being passed out, we got the older ones. We were always last in the cafeteria food line. When game equipment was passed out, it usually wasn't handed to any of us. We were never given the privilege of being captain or leader.

So although no one was physically abusive, there was that quiet snobbery. "You stay in your place and we'll leave you alone." It started in the lower grades and you learned to work around it.

You learned maybe from all of this a little more human understanding than most other people. You learned to be a bit more patient.

George R. Ariyoshi, born in Hawaii in 1926, became that state's (and the nation's) first Japanese American governor in 1973. Later on, Ariyoshi attributed his success to his father's belief in the value of an education.

Early on, my father encouraged me to attain a good education. He once told me that one can earn a fortune but that can be lost as well. An education, however, can never be taken away.

When I was an eighth grader, I told my father I wanted to become a lawyer. He was very pleased and told me he would give up everything, even the shirt off his back, in order to make my hopes possible.

That guidance and my parent's generous support have been very much responsible for my educational advancement and whatever measure of success I have been able to attain. *Okage sama de* [a traditional expression of gratitude].

Nisei children often attended a Japanese-language school as well as the American public school. The experiences were quite different. Monica Sone recalled the first day she and her brother Henry attended a Japanese school.

A man burst out of the door. His face seemed to have been carved out of granite and with turned-down mouth and nostrils flaring with disapproval, his black marble eyes crushed us into a quivering silence. This was Mr. Ohashi, the school principal....

Mother bowed deeply and murmured, "I place them in your hands."

He bowed stiffly to mother, then fastened his eyes on Henry and me and again bowed slowly and deliberately. In our

Nisei children attended Japanese-language schools like this one, where they learned Japanese customs and polite behavior as well how to read and write the Japanese language. Many Issei parents felt that they might return to Japan someday and insisted that their children be prepared for that possibility.

A Japanese-language school in Hawaii early in the 20th century. Today, many such schools still exist, attended by Sansei (third-generation) and Yonsei (fourth-generation) children whose parents wish them to preserve their knowledge of their Japanese heritage.

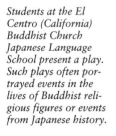

The San Gabriel Valley Judo Dojo (club) of California displays its trophy and 1932 championship banner. Judo was one of the sports Japanese immigrants brought to the United States.

haste to return the bow, we nodded our heads. With icy disdain, he snapped, "This is not an *ojigi* [bow]." He bent forward with well-oiled precision. "Bow from the waist, like this."

I wondered, if Mr. Ohashi had the nerve to criticize us in front of Mother, what more he would do in her absence....

Gradually I yielded to my double dose of schooling. Nihon Gakko was so different from [public] grammar school I found myself switching my personality back and forth daily like a chameleon. At Bailey Gatzert School I was a jumping, screaming, roustabout Yankee, but at the stroke of three when the school bell rang and doors burst open everywhere, spewing out pupils like jelly beans from a broken bag, I suddenly became a modest, faltering, earnest little Japanese girl with a small, timid voice. I trudged down a steep hill and climbed up another steep hill to Nihon Gakko with other black-haired boys and girls. On the playground, we behaved cautiously. Whenever we spied a teacher within bowing distance, we hissed at each other to stop the game, put our feet neatly together, slid our hands down to our knees and bowed slowly and sanctimoniously. In just the proper, moderate tone, putting in every ounce of respect, we chanted, "*Konichi-wa, sensei.* Good day."

A Nisei woman who grew up in a small town in California also remembered the strict discipline of the Japanese school.

They disciplined us pretty well. The one incident that I'll never forget, towards the end of the school year we always practiced for *gaku ekai*, that's graduation, the eighth grade graduation and we would all put on something. Some people would learn speeches and a lot of people had to learn something and say it. They had some plays or something like that and the teacher would have to figure it all out.... We

Students at the El Centro (California) Buddhist Church Japanese Language School present a play. Such plays often portrayed events in the lives of Buddhist religious figures or events from Japanese history.

would put on skits and we would have to polish everything up and memorize things. There was one boy that was standing up on the stage and practicing his speech. Well, in his storytelling he's supposed to say, "*Hyaku dete ike!*" (Hurry, get out!) but he said it softly…"*Hyaku dete ike!*"…quietly. And so the *sensei* (teacher) said "that's not the way to do it, you can't do it like that…" So she then yelled "*HYAKU DETE IKE!*" And you know what happened? One kid was in the basement all this while, I don't know what he was doing down there, playing when he wasn't supposed to I guess. Well, he just ran out of there and flew into the hall…because the *sensei* had yelled and he thought he was getting in trouble and you know how the *sensei* seemed to know things all the time. Oh, everyone laughed when he really ran out of there.

Some Issei parents sent their children back to Japan for an education. Such children were known as Kibei *when they returned to the United States. Tsuyoshi Horike, who was born in 1915 in Tacoma, Washington, went to Japan when he was 9, returning to the United States when he was 15. He had learned Japanese fluently, as his parents had wished, but that made it difficult for him to speak English.*

When I came back to Tacoma in 1931, I entered Central Grade School in the city. About 30 Kibei-Nisei, called back to the States as I, entered Central at the same time. I don't know what kind of criteria they used to divide us, but some of us were placed in first grade and others in second. I was enrolled in fourth. Arithmetic was very easy for me, but I couldn't pronounce the English sounds which are not in Japanese. The *f* in *food*, the *r* in *rice*, the *th* in *mouth*, and the difference between *u* and *a* in *bug* and *bag*, were impossible for me to pronounce. The teacher explained to me the position of the tongue, how to open the lips and so on, but *food* came out *hood*, however hard I tried, and I was embarrassed to death….

Some time ago I said *flied lice* for *fried rice*, to one of my white friends and he laughed at me. Even now, concerning my business, I spell *d-a-i-r-y* instead of *d-a-i-l-y* and my wife Ayako laughs. After all, I am a Kibei-Nisei who went from grade school right up through college in America and still I make these mistakes; therefore I very well understand the difficulties and pains which Issei went through who didn't have any basic English knowledge at all and after coming to the States did not go to school regularly, but instead were driven by earning a living so they had no time to study.

Isamu Noguchi

Though Isamu Noguchi became one of the most acclaimed sculptors of the 20th century, his first art teacher told him he had no talent. That teacher was Gutzon Borglum, who carved the huge stone faces of four presidents on Mount Rushmore.

Noguchi was born in Los Angeles in 1904. His father was the poet and art critic Yone Noguchi; his mother was a Caucasian American writer, Leonie Gilmore. When Noguchi was only two, his family took him to Japan, but he returned to the United States at the age of 13. After graduating from a high school in Indiana, he studied sculpture with Borglum. When he received the older man's unfavorable judgment, Noguchi enrolled at Columbia University in New York City, planning to be a doctor.

Two years later, Noguchi decided he must make another attempt to become an artist. This time, he found a more encouraging teacher, and in 1926 he won a Guggenheim Fellowship to study art in Paris. There he worked with the Romanian sculptor Constantin Brancusi, whose abstract style was a major influence on modern art.

Though many of Noguchi's own works are abstract, he worked in a variety of styles. Returning to New York in 1929, he exhibited a series of bronze heads. Collectors purchased them, and Noguchi's career was launched. In 1938, he won a commission to create a "plaque" for the Associated Press building in New York. Noguchi produced a 10-ton stainless steel image of five newspaper workers. It was the largest steel sculpture ever cast up to that time. Art critics compared it favorably to Borglum's masterpiece.

During his long and prolific career, Noguchi's art took many forms. He studied brush painting in Japan and made a huge wall mural in Mexico City. He created gardens, fountains, playgrounds, and sets for plays. At age 80, four years before his death, he designed a 102-foot-high *Bolt of Lightning* in Philadelphia to honor Benjamin Franklin. Today, his artistic legacy graces public areas all over the world.

Children, dressed as "heavenly beings," take part in a chigo *ceremony at a Buddhist temple in Hawaii in 1915. Parents took their children (aged 3, 5, and 7) to the temple to receive a blessing for health and long life. The word* chigo *means "small children."*

RELIGION

Most of the early immigrants were Buddhists. They suffered from a lack of Buddhist priests, particularly when someone was needed to recite prayers for the dead. Jusuke Okana of Kapaa, Kauai, Hawaii, wrote in the newspaper Hawaii Hochi *in 1935 about the importance of finding a priest to conduct such services.*

The bachelors were crammed four or five to a room in the camp houses and if someone were to die, the rest of the roomers were permitted to leave their work thirty minutes early in order to arrange the burial. The body was placed in a crude box and carted away to the cemetery site by mule and lowered into a hastily dug hole. No temples were there, nor priests to administer the last rites to the forgotten souls passing away on foreign soil. It was a long time later that we found out that a Mr. Tosuke Teraoka was a lay Buddhist trained to read the "Amida" sutra and the "Shoshinge." After that he was always called upon to perform the funeral services. According to my rough memory count, he must have conducted no less than 400 services.

Michiko Sato Tanaka came to the United States with her husband in 1923. She was a devout Buddhist but also followed the Japanese practice of Shinto. As an older woman, she explained to her daughter what religion had meant to her.

It is hard to become a good person by one's own strength. That's why we must draw from the strength of *kami-hotoke* [*kami*: Shinto gods; *hotoke*: Buddhas] for they are as different from humans as heaven is from earth.

There are many Buddhas but there is only one true *hotoke* [Buddha]...that is Amida Nyorai. In this world the *hotoke* who made the universe is Amida Nyorai. I have read about many religions...there are all kinds. Learning about them is like climbing a mountain: There are many different ways to climb it, but at the top is Amida Nyorai. He is like the sun. He has the power to save and sustain all living things. He said that he cannot claim to be a *hotoke* unless he could do that much....

Shinran Shonin is the one who founded the Jodo Shinshu sect—the [Buddhist] sect I belong to. He made Buddhism much easier to follow. Before, it was difficult. There were many things priests were not allowed to do. They could not eat meat, or fish, and they had to remain celibate. It was too difficult for humans to abide by. Shinran Shonin changed that. He said that as long as you have complete faith in Amida Nyorai and say *Namu Amida Butsu* even once, you will be saved, for within that single, sincere invocation is eternal salvation.

What I want to teach you is a religious way of life. A person who has religion will walk the road of Buddha's teachings:

He will find happiness. The moment you are born, you are dying. A husband dies, children grow up, but religion stays with you forever. There are times when you go astray, or times when you are very depressed, so you must greet the day with Hotokesama and *kamisama* [with Buddha and the kami, or Shinto gods].

Rose Tashiro Mitamura, who lives in New Mexico, explained the ceremonies that Buddhists conduct after death.

We followed the custom of the Buddhist religion after our mother's and father's deaths. A family representative goes to a Buddhist temple on the 49th day after the death for a memorial service. This memorial service is repeated again on the first year, the third year, and it goes on to the 13th year....

In the Tashiro home we had a room where the family worshiped. My dad had an inscribed piece of bark written by a person like a saint. It was given to my father in Japan. He was very honored and proud to have received it. He was to pass it down to the next oldest in his family, which is Harry. When Harry passes away he will pass it on to his oldest—a daughter.

When my dad was alive.... on New Year's Day we would have to get up early in the morning. He would light the candles in the room and we would bow and say a Buddhist prayer. When Buddhists visit the cemetery they burn incense at the grave. I put on flowers. The Buddhist priest comes from Denver once a year and gives a service by the tombstones at the grave site of our relatives. After the service, Harry, the oldest son, takes the priest and the family out to dinner. Buddhism isn't practiced so much here like it is in Denver where there is a large community of Japanese.

[The Nisei] ought to be brought up with the same belief as the rest of the Americans in the fatherhood of God and the brotherhood of man, if they are going to grow up and march forward shoulder to shoulder, clasping hands with their fellow Americans. Since we Christians worship the only God of heaven and earth and revere him as our spiritual Father, those of us who believe in God, therefore, have a common father.

Easter Sunday at the Japanese Methodist Episcopal Church in San Francisco around 1900. The first Japanese organization in the United States was a Christian Gospel Society in San Francisco founded by Methodist and Congregationalist student converts in 1877.

The proper observance of death was of great concern for all Japanese. Large funeral gatherings were common because there was a strong obligation for family and acquaintances to attend. Photographers were present because a photograph of the event was usually sent back to Japan to bring comfort to the deceased's family there to indicate that proper respect had been paid. Japanese custom required that relatives and friends present a koden, or funeral money gift, to help with the costs of the funeral. When Chozo Tazawa died in 1928, he was a luna on a Hawaiian plantation. Despite being well paid, a gambling habit left his wife Haruno with only 35 cents. She recalled how she paid for his Buddhist funeral:

I feel so ashamed to think that I had received so much help from friends to conduct a funeral service for my husband. I can never hold up my head again even if I'm able to afford a few luxuries now. With 35 cents, I couldn't even buy *senko* (incense) for the *hotoke-san* (the departed soul). All my friends *dashi dashi* (chipped in) for the funeral. That's the reason why I can never forget that day. Even now, I cannot indulge in luxury even if I have enough from pension money. I can't walk proudly down the street like others because of that.

Mourners gather at the funeral of an Issei pioneer in Denver in 1919.

The Reverend Shoyu Kitajima was a priest of the Jodo Sect Buddhist temple in Kapaa, Kauai, whose membership was primarily Okinawan. About 25,000 Okinawans emigrated to Hawaii between 1900 and 1924. Though Okinawa is part of Japan, its people have somewhat different customs, as Kitajima recalled.

I came to Kauai in 1938. I like the Okinawans very much and participate in their social activities. I even learned some of their folk dances. On New Year's Day here they call on each other as they do in Okinawa, carrying their jamisen [a stringed instrument] to play and sing and have a good time. I go with them, visiting one home after another. Yes, I officiate at "Senkotsu" (washing-bone ceremony) too. As you know, the Okinawans have a strong concern over their deceased family members. Their religion is deeply tied in with ancestor worship. Even if they don't attend the regular Buddhist services often, they attend memorial services without fail. They build a similar type of grave as in Okinawa with a large hall-like interior. Some have "Senkotsu" even now, usually on July 7, the Tanabata Day. They exhume the body of a deceased kin three to seven years after the first burial.... The ceremony is to exhume the body from the grave, and the closest of kin do the washing of the bones with gasoline and then put them in an earthenware pot, placing the skull on the top and sealing it for permanent burial.

A sizable number of Japanese Americans converted to Christianity, some even before they emigrated. Yoshiko Uchida recalled the importance of the Congregational Church to her family in Desert Exile.

The Japanese Independent Congregational Church of Oakland...[was] founded in 1904 by a small group of Japanese students.... In its early years it operated a dormitory that housed young Japanese students.... The church not

The Saturday school class of a Buddhist temple in Los Angeles in 1930. There, the children learned the tenets and teachings of the Buddhist religion.

only enhanced their spiritual life but also filled their need for an ethnic community. As the Issei began to marry and raise families, it continued to be a focal point in their lives, providing support and a sense of community. Indeed it was almost an extended family, with each member caring and concerned about the lives of others.

My parents were among the earliest members of this Japanese church and never missed attending services on Sunday. Consequently, my sister and I never missed going to Sunday School unless we were sick.

While Keiko and I were still having our toast and steaming cups of cocoa on Sunday mornings, Mama would cook a large pot of rice to be eaten with the food she had prepared the night before. When it was cooked, she took it to her bed and bundled it up in a thick quilt to keep warm until we got home from church with a carload of people who had no place to go for Sunday dinner....

The Sunday School service was conducted in English, and all the children met together in the chapel to sing hymns, reading the words from large cloth pages that hung from a metal stand. "Open your mouths," my father would encourage us. "Let me hear you sing as loud as you can!" And we would oblige by bellowing out, "Jesus loves me this I know, for the Bible tells me so...."

The adult service was conducted entirely in Japanese and usually lasted well over an hour, as long hymns droned on and on to the accompaniment of a wheezing reed organ. The minister delivered lengthy sermons which my father admitted to finding extremely tedious. But he added to the length of the service himself since, as one of the deacons, he made the weekly announcements and, once he began talking, found it difficult to be brief.

A bon festival at the Seattle Buddhist Church in the 1930s. During the three-day bon feast, from July 13 to 15, the spirits of the dead are welcomed back to earth by their relatives. These children were dressed for Obon odori, folk dances to welcome the spirits.

A viper is nonetheless a viper wherever the egg is hatched—so a Japanese American, born of Japanese parents—grows up to be a Japanese, not an American.

—*Los Angeles Times*, 1942

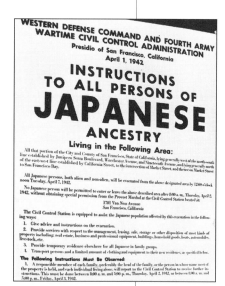

After President Roosevelt issued Executive Order 9066 in February 1942, posters such as this one appeared throughout Japanese American communities. Japanese Americans were ordered to report to a Civil Control Station on a given date to receive instructions on their "evacuation."

INTERNMENT AND WAR

Usaburo Katamoto emigrated to Hawaii from Nakajima, Japan, in 1910. At the time of the Pearl Harbor attack, he was working in Honolulu. At the age of 82, he recalled that fateful day.

It was Sunday, December 7. Morning time. We were supposed to get first-aid graduation at that Kokusai Theater. The Japanese community—mostly elders—been taking first-aid lesson for about a month, I think. We were just about to graduate so I went to the theater. Then the graduate ceremony don't start because, you know, plenty fires on; they say that enemy plane. We felt that the Japanese attack but we didn't want to say, you know.

Somebody says, "No that's the U.S. Army taking a target practice." Well, it didn't look like that. It's more like real stuff, you know. Then a plane came from Diamond Head side of town and went over the city. It came right over Aala Market which is near the theater. We can see, you know.

Some says, "Eh, that plane don't look like United States' plane 'cause the body is shorter than United States' one. A different shape." We can see that Japanese flag mark on the body. So you know it's got to be real attack.

At an assembly center, Japanese Americans receive instructions on how to obtain transportation to one of the relocation camps.

The news of the attack on Pearl Harbor shocked Japanese Americans wherever they lived. Yo Nigata, a California resident, remembered her feelings.

I had gone to a Nisei basketball game in Oakland when the attack was announced. I guess I didn't quite believe it, or I wasn't quite sure of its significance. Anyway, I went to a movie that afternoon with Mort [her future husband]. They kept interrupting it with announcements of the attack and calls for all Navy personnel to report to their ships. Then I began to feel frightened...and guilty. As if I personally had something to do with it.

Toru Matsumoto was living in New York City with his American wife, Emma, when the attack on Pearl Harbor took place. He would be interned as an enemy alien for the duration of the war.

In the elevator a neighbor spoke to me.
"Mr. Matsumoto, your country has attacked us."
I did not quite hear what she said, and begged her pardon.
"I say, Japan has attacked America."
I still could not believe that I had heard her correctly, but when I opened the door of our apartment I saw Emma at the radio.
"Papa, it's war," she said. "Hawaii is under attack."
So it was true!... I sat near the radio and listened to bulletin after dreadful bulletin. With every word one more of my hopes was shattered....
The telephone began to ring with calls from friends who wanted to know whether they could help us. There was nothing to be done, but I was glad to know that my friends were still my friends. At twelve o'clock we decided to go to bed, and I was just getting into my pajamas when the doorbell rang. Emma opened the door.
Two plain-clothes men pushed into the room.
"Are you Toru Matsumoto?"
"Yes."
"You are under arrest, by the order of the President of the United States."

Frank Chuman, who would later serve as the president of the Japanese American Citizens League, was a student at the University of California at Los Angeles law school in 1941. He heard the news of the bombing of Pearl Harbor on the radio on his way home from church. His parents decided that it would be wise to destroy any evidence of lingering family ties to Japan.

My father went to a dresser in his bedroom where he kept two *samurai* swords, one long for two hands, the other short. These were family treasures which had been handed down to him. His ancestors had been *samurai*, warriors of the Satsuma clan. I had looked forward to owning these swords some day, and many times had secretly taken them out to admire the magnificent blades. My father removed the swords from the beautiful inlaid cases and he and I

U.S. soldiers escort an elderly couple from their home in Seattle. No one, young or old, was spared from removal to the camps. Anyone of Japanese descent was treated as potentially disloyal.

Children were bewildered when they had to leave their homes abruptly, taking only what their families could carry.

The father of the Mochida family forces a brave smile for the photographer as his family left for the camps. But seeing his children tagged like luggage must have been insulting and humiliating.

People arriving at the Heart Mountain, Wyoming, Relocation Center in August 1942. They would be housed in shoddy barracks for the next three years. There, they would endure winters marked by temperatures that fell to 30 degrees below zero.

took them out into the back yard. There he thrust both blades, bare and glistening, deep into the ground and we buried them. I was sad and disconsolate. Disposal of these beautiful pieces of Japanese workmanship seemed to be a symbolic rite. It was as though a tangible cultural tie with Japan was being severed.

Later, I drove to Japanese town [in Los Angeles], to see what was going on. It was like a ghost town. I felt very conscious of the fact that I had a Japanese face. I wondered how we would be treated by our non-Japanese friends and neighbors. I felt very much alone, silently hoping for some words of comfort but fearing that my features would cause me to be the target of hatred and suspicion for what the Japanese Navy had done.

Kyoko Oshima Takayanagi, the daughter of Japanese immigrants, was born in Oakland, California, in 1924. She described the results of the Pearl Harbor bombing on her community.

We were living in rural areas in California when the war broke out.... Living on the coast you'd have blackout curtains on your windows and all of this stuff [so that if enemy bombers attacked, they could not see lights on the ground]. And the Japanese had curfews. We had to be in off the streets by nine o'clock, in our homes. The Chinese wore pins, "I am Chinese."...

My parents didn't know what was going to hit. Then my father, as an alien, had to get permits to go [a certain distance from his home]. I forget what the distance was. He was having trouble making money.... Absolute strangers would yell, "Get the hell to Yokohama!" "Get the hell off the streets!"

Seichi Hayashida was living near Seattle, Washington, when President Roosevelt issued Executive Order No. 9066, which called for the internment of Japanese Americans. Hayashida recalled his reaction to the news.

I was really disillusioned I guess would be the word you'd use. I never expected to be evacuated. At least without being charged of something. You know, the army came and said within two weeks, pack a suitcase and one duffle bag and be at this railroad siding twelve o'clock sharp on a certain day, and get your affairs in order, they didn't tell us how long we'd be gone or when we could expect to get back.... I lived in a little community of about 50 families.... But one day we were all there, and the next day at noon they were gone, no Japanese Americans left in this town. I lived in Bellevue, Washington.

The assembly center at Tanforan, California, had previously been a racetrack. Charles Kikuchi recalled his first days there in May 1942, an experience he chronicled in his diary.

The whole family pitched in to build our new home at Tanforan. We raided the Clubhouse and tore off the linoleum from the bar table and put it on our floor so that it now looks rather homelike. Takeshi [his brother, also called Tom] works pretty hard for a little guy and makes himself useful, but the gals are not so useful. They'd rather wander around looking for the boys. However, they pitched in and helped clean up the new messhall so that we could have our meals there instead of walking all the way over to the clubhouse. It's about 11:00 [P.M.] now and everyone has gone to bed. You can hear the voices all the way down the barracks—everything sounds so clear. Tom just stepped out to water his "victory garden." The community spirit is picking up rapidly and everyone seems willing to pitch in. They had a meeting tonight to get volunteers for cooks and waiters at the new messhall and this was done without difficulty. Rules were also made for each barracks such as radio off at 10:00 and not too many lights so that the fuse would not get overloaded....

I saw a soldier in a tall guardhouse near the barbed wire fence and did not like it because it reminds me of a concentration camp.

A few Japanese Americans in Hawaii shared the experience of being rounded up as potentially dangerous enemies. Some of them, like Gladys Miura Sodetani and her family, were shipped to camps in the mainland United States. In 1976, Sodetani made a list of the things she remembered about her experiences.

I REMEMBER:
The military police knocking on our door in the middle of the night on December 7 and taking my father away.

The rough voyages on boats from Maui to Oahu and from Oahu to California; being so seasick I could eat no food for five days except sucking on oranges.

The canned green beans which I disliked at the Immigration Center.

The long train ride from California to Arkansas and my little sister and I playing on the Pullman [sleeping car] bed.

Looking out of our barrack window and seeing snow for the first time.

Wearing galoshes, woolen mittens, snow caps, earmuffs that my mother had knitted.

The big stove in the middle of our room to keep us warm.

The men going out into the forest to gather firewood and their stories of all the snakes they encountered.

The tall, handsome teacher who daily read aloud to us *Tales of King Arthur and His Knights of the Round Table* and who also held math speed contests.

Moving to dry, hot Arizona.... Cooling the room with an electric fan placed in a frame....

Sitting on our blankets under the stars on rocky buttes to watch movies such as "I'll Be Seeing You", starring Ginger Rogers.

After the war, standing on the deck of our boat in the calm Pacific Ocean in November, 1945, and seeing the island of Oahu and feeling so happy to be back in Hawaii again!...

I REMEMBER.

At the relocation camp in Manzanar, California, shown here, guards fired on a crowd of protestors, killing two, in December 1942. Starting in 1969, Japanese Americans in California have made an annual pilgrimage to Manzanar to remember the unjust detention of Japanese Americans during World War II.

An Armistice Day celebration in November 1942 at the Gila River, Arizona, relocation camp. Armistice Day commemorated the service of U.S. veterans of World War I. In fact, some elderly Japanese Americans who served in the U.S. Army and Navy during that war were now incarcerated in the detention camps.

In the 1980s, Akiyo Deloyd testified before a Congressional committee about her experiences in the camp at Poston, Arizona.

When we arrived in camp, what I saw was complete desolation. A camp in the middle of the desert; a barbed wire fence surrounding the entire camp with an armed sentry at each gate; no paved roads, only heat and dust storms. If this was not a complete prison-like atmosphere, I will leave it to members of the committee to tell me what they would consider it was if they were 19 years old.

We lived in a bare room, seven of us, five children and our parents. No separate partitions for my parents. Our bedding—we filled canvas bags with hay. I can remember how the hay pricked through the canvas as I slept. I felt this to be especially demeaning and degrading.

In addition, I was told that one member of the family had to work in the kitchen in order for the family to eat. This frightened me, so I did not hesitate for one second to work as a waitress. My monthly salary was $16 for eight hours a day, seven days a week.

My mother died in Poston, Arizona. She was a diabetic. I can remember the time that I went to the kitchen for milk. I was told the milk was for babies and small children. The diet of rice, macaroni, and potato was hardly a suitable diet for a diabetic. As far as that goes, it was not an adequate diet for anyone.

In a way, the stress of going into camp, poor diet, and worry hastened the death of my mother. She was 52 years old. She had to be cremated; there was no choice. My sorrow that I have to this day is that I could not put a fresh flower on her grave. All our flowers were made of Kleenex.

Yuri Kochiyama was born and grew up in San Pedro, California. She was sent to the internment camp in Jerome, Arkansas. Years later, she described life there.

When we got to Jerome, Arkansas, we were shocked because we had never seen an area like it. There was forest all around us. And they told us to wait till the rains hit. This would not only turn into mud, but Arkansas swamp lands. That's where they put us—in swamp lands, surrounded by forests. It was nothing like California....

There were army-type barracks, with 200 to 205 people to each block and every block had its own mess hall, facility for washing clothes, showering. It was all surrounded by barbed wire, and armed soldiers. I think they said only seven people were killed in total, though thirty were shot, because they went too close to the fence. Where we were, nobody thought of escaping because you'd be more scared of the swamps—the poisonous snakes, the bayous.... Although Arkansas is in the South, the winters were very, very cold. We had a pot-bellied stove in every room and we burned wood. Everything was very organized. We got there in October, and were warned to prepare ourselves. So on our block, for instance, males eighteen

Crowded into small barracks rooms, Japanese Americans did their best to make them seem as much like a normal home as possible.

In an attempt to maintain their community life, Japanese Americans in the camps opened schools, published newspapers, and organized social events. Here, a musical group known as the Mikados (an old name for the Japanese emperor) played swing music at a dance at the Minidoka, Idaho, camp.

100

and over could go out into the forest to chop down trees for wood for the winter. The men would bring back the trees, and the women sawed the trees. Everybody worked. The children would pile up the wood for each unit....

For instance, the roofers would come by, and everyone would hunger for information from the outside world. We wanted to know what was happening with the war. We weren't allowed to bring radios; that was contraband. And there were no televisions then. So we would ask the workers to bring us back some papers, and they would give us papers from Texas or Arkansas, so for the first time we would find out about news from the outside.

Seichi and Chiyeko Hayashida lived in Seattle, Washington, until the outbreak of World War II. They were first sent to Tule Lake camp, where they married, and then transferred to the Minidoka camp in Idaho, where their first child was born. An interviewer in Idaho in 1989 recorded their story. Seichi began:

My son, I have a son that was born in 1944 at the Minidoka Center.
Chiyeko: Oh yes, it was snowing that day.
Seichi: His middle name is Yukio, which means snow boy.

CH: The name means—is a different meaning—but Yuki in Japanese is snow, Yuki, Yukio means straight as an arrow. And that's why we named him that.

SH: It snowed great big inch flakes, and we had to walk through that snow and mud for about a mile. I lived on one end of the camp, and the hospital was outside the camp property, right near the entrance so. And the wind was coming against me on the way up to the hospital, and I went to get [the doctor] and that's on the way up I said I'm going to name him Yukio, using the word Yuki meaning snow. He never uses it, just uses the initial.

CH: Well, I was 2 weeks overdue so I walked to the hospital and I had to wait until, well they induced, they gave me castor oil. And naturally the baby was ready to come when everybody was gone to early supper.

George Sakamoto was born in Sacramento County, California, in the 1920s and spent time in two internment camps.

They relocated us in a permanent camp at a place called Tule Lake, near Marysville. It was half swamp and half desert. If you went there now you would say, "Don't tell me people lived here." It looked like an old-style army camp. There were common bathrooms, showers, washrooms, and mess hall. Each family was thrown in one room, whether it had two people or eight.

We were fed things we weren't accustomed to. Beef brains, tongue, kidneys and liver were the mainstay of the kitchens. We had very few Japanese staples. Rice and certain meats were hauled out of the warehouse before they got to our kitchen,

A photographer recorded the treasured items on one woman's bureau in a camp: a portrait of her son in the army, letters from him, a religious picture, and a potted plant.

Mealtime in a camp was a family occasion, but it was also a daily reminder that life was not the same as it had been in their real homes. The barbed wire surrounding the camps was clear evidence that those within were prisoners—jailed indefinitely merely because of their race.

The all-Nisei 442nd Regimental Combat Team fought heroically in Italy and France during World War II, becoming the most decorated unit of its size and length of service in U.S. military history.

Yasuo Kenmotsu was killed in combat during World War II in the service of the United States.

because some of the administrators were saying, "Hell, we don't get enough meat. Why should we feed it to these concentration camp people?"

We had a pig farm and a chicken farm to raise meat for the camp. Then, because we had so much idle time, there were courses we could take. A lot of people learned something there. Women learned crocheting and making brooches. Other people made shelves and tables. Sometimes they exchanged things they made.

In September 1943 we were reassigned to a camp in Colorado. Our son, Gary, had just been born, but they wanted to separate the family. We fought it, and finally they decided to send us together. We were put on a train with the shades drawn. There were two armed guards at each end of the car. Even when we had to go to the bathroom we were restricted. It was hot, no air conditioning. We couldn't see daylight or night. We only knew we had reached our destination when we were told to get out. That's all. I would say we were shipped like a bunch of cattle....

Colorado was much like the first camp, but it was a real dust bowl. You constantly had to protect your face from the dust. When you looked out and saw a dust storm coming you just had to hide and cover your face with a wet cloth. It was an awful place.

Jeanne Wakatsuki wrote a book entitled Farewell to Manzanar *about her experiences at the Manzanar camp in California.*

As the months at Manzanar turned to years, it became a world unto itself, with its own logic and familiar ways.... In most ways it was a totally equipped American small town, complete with schools, churches, Boy Scouts, beauty parlors, neighborhood gossip, fire and police departments, glee clubs, softball leagues, Abbott and Costello movies, tennis courts, and traveling shows....

In our family, while Papa puttered, Mama made her daily rounds to the mess halls, helping young mothers with their feeding, planning diets for the various ailments people suffered from. She wore a bright yellow, longbilled sun hat she had made herself and always kept stiffly starched. Afternoons I would see her coming from blocks away, heading home, her tiny figure warped by heat waves and that bonnet a yellow flower wavering in the glare.

In their disagreement over serving the country, Woody and Papa had struck a kind of compromise. Papa talked him out of volunteering; Woody waited for the army to induct him. Meanwhile he clerked in the co-op general store. Kiyo, nearly thirteen by this time, looked forward to the heavy winds. They moved the sand around and uncovered obsidian arrowheads he could sell to old men in camp for fifty cents apiece. Ray, a few years older, played in the six-man touch football league, sometimes against Caucasian teams who would come in from Lone Pine or Independence. My sister Lillian was in high school and singing with a hillbilly band called the Sierra Stars—jeans, cowboy hats, two guitars, and a tub bass. And my oldest brother, Bill, led a dance band called The Jive Bombers—brass and rhythm, with cardboard fold-out music stands lettered J.B. Dances were held every weekend in one of the recreation halls. Bill played trumpet and took vocals on Glenn Miller [a popular band leader of the time] arrangements of such tunes as *In the Mood*, *String of Pearls*, and *Don't Fence Me In*. He didn't sing *Don't Fence Me In* out of protest, as if trying quietly to mock the authorities. It just happened to be a hit song one year, and they all wanted to be an up-to-date American swing band. They would blast it out into recreation barracks full of bobby-soxed, jitterbugging couples:

> *Oh, give me land lots of land*
> *Under starry skies above,*
> *Don't fence me in.*
> *Let me ride through the wide*
> *Open country that I love.*

The all-Nisei 442nd Regimental Combat Team was created in 1943. Some of its members had originally served in the Hawaii National Guard. Among them was Spark M. Matsunaga, later a U.S. senator from Hawaii. He recalled the reaction of the residents immediately after the Pearl Harbor attack on Hawaii.

When an invasion of Hawaiian Islands was believed imminent, all Americans regardless of race stood side by side in beach dugouts and trenches, fully prepared to repel the enemy. After the battle of Midway in June, 1942, when invasion by the enemy became a more remote matter, our fellow Americans suddenly turned to us of Japanese ancestry and looked at us with a suspicious eye, almost as if to say, "Why, he's a Jap!" It was shortly thereafter that all of us of Japanese ancestry who were in American uniform were given orders to turn in our arms and ammunition and were corralled at Schofield Barracks, an Army post about 22 miles northwest of Honolulu.

Before we had any chance to bid goodbye to our loved ones, we found ourselves on board troopship sailing God-knew-where. Speculation was rife that we were headed for a concentration camp....

We pictured ourselves as a battalion of forced laborers. As time went on, we were put through close-order drill and trained with wooden guns. We wrote home of our great desire for combat duty to prove our loyalty to the United States. It was not known to us then that our letters were being censored by higher authority. We learned subsequently that because of the tenor of our letters, the War Department decided to give us a chance. Our guns were returned to us, and were told that we were going to be prepared for combat duty.... Grown men leaped with joy on learning that they were finally going to be given the chance on the field of battle to prove their loyalty to the land of their birth.

Daniel K. Inouye

In 1973, Senator Daniel K. Inouye was named to the special Senate committee that investigated Watergate—the scandal surrounding the illegal activities of President Richard Nixon's campaign committee. Though Inouye had been a senator for more than 10 years, few Americans outside Hawaii had ever heard of him. Inouye was thrust into the national spotlight when a lawyer for one of Nixon's aides publicly referred to him as "that little Jap." Typically, Inouye shrugged off the offensive slur. He had overcome far greater obstacles in a lifetime of service to his country.

Born to immigrant parents in Honolulu in 1924, Inouye hoped to become a doctor. In 1943, however, he left the University of Hawaii to enlist in the 442nd Regimental Combat Team. In his autobiography, he remembered the enthusiasm of its members: "In maneuvers against the 69th Division, the 442nd was assigned the role of Aggressor Force, which meant that we were only supposed to provide the opposition while the 69th, three times our strength, polished up its tactical skills. I guess we didn't follow the script or something, because by the time the exercise ended, the umpires were forced to rule that we had 'wiped out' two of the Friendly Force's three regiments."

Two years later, Inouye led his platoon in an attack on a German infantry post. Though wounded in one arm and both legs, he hurled grenades into three German machine-gun nests. He won three medals for the action, but his right arm was amputated, ending his plans for a medical career.

In the postwar years, Inouye completed his college education and earned advanced degrees in law. After returning to Hawaii, he entered politics and served several terms in the territorial legislature. In 1959, when Hawaii became the 50th state, Inouye became the first Japanese American ever elected to the House of Representatives. Three years later, he won election to the U.S. Senate.

Inouye, who had experienced racial discrimination as a child, backed the civil rights legislation and social welfare programs of the 1960s. Since then, Hawaiians have elected him to the Senate for five more terms.

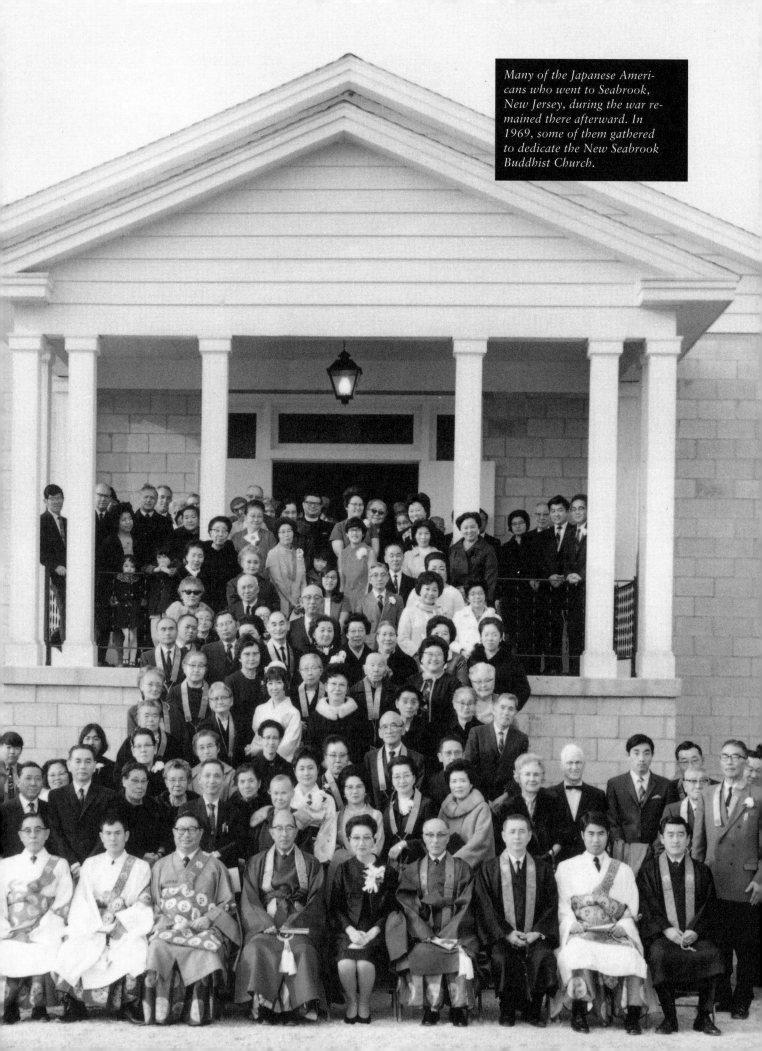

Many of the Japanese Americans who went to Seabrook, New Jersey, during the war remained there afterward. In 1969, some of them gathered to dedicate the New Seabrook Buddhist Church.

CHAPTER SIX

PART OF AMERICA

On July 15, 1946, veterans of the 442nd Regimental Combat Team assembled on the White House lawn. In his greeting, President Harry Truman said, "You fought not only the enemy but you fought prejudice—and you have won." However, the many wounds caused by the wartime internment of Japanese Americans took decades to heal.

The last of the concentration camps on the mainland did not close until seven months after the end of World War II. Indeed, some elderly Issei had to be forced to leave the camps, for they feared the reception they would face outside. The War Relocation Authority gave each Japanese American who left the camps just $25 to start a new life.

Many Japanese American internees wanted to return to their old homes, but on arriving there, they often faced the same hostility as before. Many found it impossible to reclaim their homes and businesses and had to begin anew as farm laborers and servants.

During the war, some camp internees had accepted the offer to resettle in other parts of the United States. About 10 percent of them went to work for the Seabrook Farms Company in New Jersey. A producer of frozen and canned foods, Seabrook actively recruited Japanese Americans from the detention camps, for they proved to be reliable workers. After the war, some of these and other Japanese Americans who had relocated remained in their new homes. For the first time, sizable Japanese American communities existed outside the western states.

Another group of Nisei, who had accepted a government offer to give up their United States citizenship, fought to revoke this renunciation after the war ended. (In view of the way they were treated, it is surprising that only about 6,000 Nisei chose this form of protest.) About 5,500 Nisei successfully regained their American citizenship.

There were other hopeful signs. In the 1946 election in California, voters rejected a proposal to make the 1913 Alien Land Act part of the state constitution. In 1952, the California Supreme Court ruled that the Alien Land Act was unconstitutional, although similar laws remained on the books in other states until the 1960s.

In 1946, the Japanese American Citizens League sent Mike Masaoka, a veteran of the 442nd Regimental Combat Team, to Washington as a lobbyist. Partly through Masaoka's efforts, President Truman signed a 1948 law that provided compensation to Japanese Americans for the property they lost in the evacuation. However, the average compensation was only $450, and the last of the claims was not processed until 1965. By then many of the people who filed them had died.

The most important postwar legislative victory came in 1952, when Congress finally ended the legal bar to citizenship for Asian immigrants. For thousands of Issei, it was the fulfillment of a dream, the end of being made to feel "unworthy" of becoming Americans. By 1965, about 46,000 of them had become citizens of the land where they had lived for decades. As one wrote:

With the certificate of
naturalization
In my hand
I buy a tombstone next.

In the postwar years, Japanese Americans also made considerable gains in the American territory of Hawaii. In 1946 the sugar-plantation workers united in the first industrywide strike in Hawaii's history. After 79 days, the owners gave in to the workers' demands. Three years later, the International Longshoremen's and Warehousemen's Union (ILWU) organized Japanese workers in Hawaii in a strike that lasted 177 days before a wage increase was won.

These two strikes signaled that Japanese Hawaiians were no longer willing to accept the second-class status they had held in the past. As Daniel K. Inouye, a decorated war veteran who became a lawyer and later a U.S. senator, wrote: "The time had come for us to step forward. We had fought for that right with all the furious patriotism in our bodies, and now we didn't want to go back to the plantation....We wanted to take our full place in society."

In the Hawaiian territorial elections of 1954, many young Nisei ran on the Democratic ticket against the long-entrenched Republican party of the islands. The Democrats captured both houses of the Hawaiian legislature, where nearly half of the new delegates were Japanese Americans.

That victory spurred the movement to make Hawaii a state. In 1959, that goal was achieved, and Inouye became the first Asian American to win election to the House of Representatives. Three years later, Inouye was elected to the Senate, another "first" for Japanese Americans. Patsy Takemoto Mink, the first Japanese American female lawyer in Hawaii, won a seat in Congress in 1964, becoming the first Asian American woman to serve there. George Ariyoshi served as Hawaii's governor from 1973 to 1986.

Japanese Americans on the mainland also won political victories. Norman Mineta, a Nisei who had been an internee in the Heart Mountain camp in Wyoming, was first elected to Congress from California in 1974, the first of many terms. Californians also sent S. I.

Hayakawa, the conservative president of San Francisco State College, to the U.S. Senate in 1976.

In the 1960s, the third generation of Japanese Americans, the Sansei, started to become active in political affairs. Some took part in the student protests against the Vietnamese War; others were inspired by the efforts of another American minority group, African

The Immigration and Nationality Act of 1952 made it possible for Asian immigrants to obtain U.S. citizenship for the first time. Many Issei, such as this group in San Francisco in 1953, accepted the offer.

Americans, to win full rights as citizens.

Though most Sansei no longer spoke Japanese fluently, they maintained a strong sense of pride in their heritage—but with a modern viewpoint. When they first learned of the forced internment, their reaction was to ask their parents and grandparents, "How could you have let this happen?" A generation removed from the camp experience, the Sansei grew up in a time when mass demonstrations as a form of protest was commonplace. The fact that the Issei and Nisei had peacefully accepted in-

ternship was hard for them to understand.

After the 1960s, barriers against minority groups fell in schools, housing, and the workplace. Japanese Americans took advantage of their new opportunities. Sansei and their children, the Yonsei, enrolled in large numbers in prestigious American colleges, where the traditional Japanese respect for education served them well.

Japanese Americans have become successful lawyers, doctors, scientists, artists, and business leaders. Minoru Yamasaki, born in Seattle, founded an architectural firm that designed such buildings as the World Trade Center. Los Angeles-born Isamu Noguchi became a multitalented sculptor, painter, and theatrical set designer before his death in 1988. Garrett Hongo, a Hawaii-born Yonsei, is a noted poet and playwright. Ellison Shoji Onizuka was one of the astronauts who lost their lives in the *Challenger* disaster in 1986. Kristi Yamaguchi, the Olympic gold medalist in women's figure skating in 1992, has won both national and world championships in her sport. Hiroshima, a group of Sansei musicians, has recorded many popular albums of its blend of traditional Japanese music and American jazz.

However, the very success of Japanese Americans has caused some concern. Only a few decades ago, Japanese Americans were stereotyped in the movies as servants or "inscrutable" Asians. Today, they face a different kind of stereotype: the "model minority" that excels in school, has no crime problem, and is destined for a high-tech, high-paying job. Japanese American children endure pressure to live up to this stereotype.

In addition, the success of Japan itself as an economic superpower and competitor with the United States has affected Japanese Americans. Anti-Japanese prejudice, and sometimes violence, is often directed against anyone who has Japanese features.

On the other hand, many Americans have found much to value in the cultural contributions of Japanese Americans. Elegant Japanese styles have influenced modern art and architecture. Many Americans of all races now study the various Japanese martial arts, such as judo and karate. Growing miniature bonsai trees, an ancient art in Japan, has become a popular American hobby. Japanese food, such as sushi and sashimi, appeals to health-conscious Americans. Zen and other forms of Buddhism, with their emphasis on contemplation and inner peace, have a growing number of followers in the United States. Recent immigrants from Japan have tended to be artists, designers, and students seeking the freer society of the United States.

Many Japanese American cultural societies still celebrate the traditional holidays and keep alive the ancient traditions. In 1934, residents of Los Angeles's Little Tokyo held the first Nisei Week, an annual celebration of Japanese American heritage. Stopped during the war, the event was revived in 1949. Today San Francisco and Honolulu have similar festivals.

For many Japanese Americans, true acceptance did not come until the redress movement, which aimed to redress, or make up for, the suffering of those interned in camps during World War II. In 1976, the JACL set up the National Committee for Redress to study the issue. Other local redress

Three generations of the Hada family—from Pennsylvania, Texas, and New Jersey—gather for a photograph in Bridgeton, New Jersey, in 1967.

groups were formed in Seattle, Los Angeles, and Chicago. In 1980, Congress responded by establishing a commission to investigate the treatment of Japanese Americans during World War II.

The following year, Peter Irons, a legal historian, discovered that the government had deliberately suppressed evidence in the wartime trials of Fred Korematsu and two other Nisei convicted of violating the relocation orders. Three Sansei lawyers took up the cases and filed petitions to have the convictions overturned. Korematsu and Gordon Hirabayashi won their cases; the third member of the group died before the court could rule on his petition.

The congressional commission invited former internees to give testimony on what they had experienced. Elderly Japanese Americans, many of whom had long wanted to put those years behind them, now stepped forward to tell their stories. At last the suffering and humiliation of the internees became a public issue. The commission's final report, entitled *Personal Justice Denied*, indicated its sympathy for redress.

In 1988, Congress passed a bill authorizing payments of $20,000 to each of the surviving internees. President Ronald Reagan signed the bill on August 10. It took two years before the first payments were made to the oldest living survivors of the American concentration camps.

It was a notable victory, won after many years of struggle, and Japanese Americans of all generations celebrated. Their country had at last acknowledged that it had wronged them.

Each check for $20,000 came with a printed letter of apology that stated: "A monetary sum and words alone cannot restore lost years or erase painful memories; neither can they fully convey our Nation's resolve to rectify injustice and to uphold the rights of individuals. We can never fully right the wrongs of the past. But we can take a clear stand for justice and recognize that serious injustices were done to Japanese Americans during World War II."

Members of the Japanese American Citizens League lay a wreath at the Tomb of the Unknown Soldier at Arlington National Cemetery in 1960.

Thanksgiving Day at a Japanese American hostel in Philadelphia in 1949. After the war ended and the internment camps closed, the first impulse of most Japanese Americans was to put the past behind them and resume normal lives.

STARTING OVER

Yoshiko Uchida spent part of the war years in the Topaz internment camp in Utah. She described her feelings upon leaving.

I left Topaz determined to work hard and prove I was as loyal as any other American. I felt a tremendous sense of responsibility to make good, not just for myself, but for all Japanese Americans. I felt I was representing all the Nisei, and it was sometimes an awesome burden to bear.

When the war was over, the brilliant record of the highly decorated Nisei combat teams, and favorable comments of the GIs returning from Japan, helped alleviate to some degree the hatred directed against the Japanese Americans during the war.

Born in California, George Sakamoto spent time during World War II in the Tule Lake and Granada internment camps. The government offered to let him look for a place to relocate his family, which wound up in Seabrook, New Jersey.

Seabrook came to my attention on a train from Chicago to New York. I read in the *Reader's Digest* that Seabrook had gotten government contracts to furnish food for the army and that they were looking for help. I was traveling with a friend. When we got to New York we inquired at the Work Relocation Authority and were told Seabrook was especially interested in people from the detention camps.

We were brought to Seabrook from the WRA office in Philadelphia, and we took a tour of the plant. The people were very nice, I thought. We were told that they would furnish rent-free housing. There was a school right here, and the system wasn't bad. Water and electricity came with the house. The company would provide transportation to work, and would even furnish pots and pans....

It hasn't been bad here. Many Japanese families came here with practically nothing, and now their children are well educated and are doctors and lawyers. The Japanese have done well here. The people in New Jersey were more tolerant and understanding than those in California.

Teddy Yoshikami recalled growing up in Seabrook.

I was born in the camps, actually. Tule Lake. From Tule Lake our family went to Seabrook. I pretty much was raised in Seabrook, through high school. I grew up in this little village. Most of the people who lived there worked in the plant, the Seabrook Frozen Foods Plant, and so it was like this little company town, I'd guess you'd call it. So there was a Seabrook School, Seabrook Day Care, a Seabrook Community

House, even an infirmary for a while, where if you had medical problems you could go there. In the community center we had a library, community activities, movies, social events. The Christian church would have their services there. The Buddhist church always had its own separate building.

After leaving the internment camps, many Japanese families found that no property remained in their former homes. Seichi Haya-shida and his family returned briefly to Washington State in 1945. He told an interviewer in 1989:

I went back in '45 [to Washington] to see what was left of my property, and everything was gone. What I had left with the man who I thought was a friend, had known for a long time, all my adult life, he wasn't there, and all the stuff I left there in his care [was now owned by another family]. This man shows me a government bill of sale for all the stuff I left...farm equipment, tools, household goods...so I had nothing to go back to.

Usaburo Katamoto was interned in Santa Fe, New Mexico. After the war, he returned to Hawaii.

When I get home, it was good to see the family. [A] few of my friends and my kids and wife was waiting at the pier. We shake hand and it was good. But was just—nothing special. We expected all those things.

The only thing I felt was that we lost a good three years. In fact, three years and ten months. Almost four years, eh? When I come back I see all my friends made big money and sitting pretty. During the wartime, they all was willing to work, you know. They made easy money and sure made good fortune. But I was out for that time.

Let's see, I got back in November. Then, I was thinking going back to my own boat building business again, but the materials was limited and the wholesalers don't supply new openers like me. They got to supply their own customers. So I says, "I no sense open." My boat building days were over.

A chigo *celebration at the Seabrook, New Jersey, Buddhist Church in 1957. The ceremony dates from the Kamakura period (1138–1333), when Japanese nobles sent their children to temples to receive an education. The costumes worn by the children are similar to the clothing of Japanese nobles 800 years ago.*

With the passage of the McCarren-Walter Act in 1952, Japanese immigrants became eligible for citizenship. Many elderly Issei filed their applications. One of them, Kiyoko Nieda, wrote a poem:

> Going steadily to study English,
> Even through the rain at night,
> I thus attain,
> Late in life,
> American citizenship.

Japanese American sushi restaurants, like this one in Philadelphia, have become popular for their emphasis on natural foods served in an attractive manner. It takes years of training for a person to become adept at preparing sushi. Another popular Japanese food is tempura—small pieces of fish, meat, or vegetables that are coated with batter and fried.

SUCCESS AND REDRESS

Through perseverance, many Japanese Americans overcame the prejudice against them. A Nisei woman described her years of struggle.

When I came to UCLA (1936) I had to pick a college major so I chose elementary education. I always wanted to be a teacher, so even when they told me there would never be a job for me, I went ahead to work for my teacher's certificate. Actually, some of the other girls were in sociology or economics and they'd never be able to get a job either. So I guess you can say we were all even.

After I got my degree in 1940, I didn't even look for a job in teaching since there were no openings for Japanese. Soon after, I was evacuated. While in camp, they needed teachers very badly and somehow or other, they knew I had teacher training and the state sent over a teaching certificate. So I taught for several years in camp—when I relocated to Idaho, that state kept after me to teach.

I came back to California in 1946 and tried to find a teaching job. It was still discouraging but I stuck to it and finally landed a position. I still remember that first day...as I was walking into the teacher's lunchroom, one of the teachers said in a voice loud enough so that I could hear, "Look who we're hiring now, we really must be hard up."

It wasn't a pleasant situation but I knew I could teach and my experiences in camp helped out. Now that I look back on it, I always wanted to teach, I finally got the opportunity, and I'm glad I stuck it out.

Natsu Okuyama Ozawa emigrated to the United States in 1924. In the late 1970s, she spoke with pride of her family's accomplishments.

My older son, he can read Japanese. He can speak quite nice Japanese, but the younger one, I tried to teach him at home after school, but you know how hard to keep up the children studying the foreign language at home. Can't read, write, but he speaks nicely.

The first one lived near the San Fernando Valley. Now he is working at the Los Angeles aircraft company. The second one finished medicine and now in Sacramento. Has office there. I have six grandchildren. [Laughs.] There's one that's second year of college. Now, these days, have the trouble with the young boys and girls. They were no trouble at all. I was lucky to raise children at that time. [Laughs.]

There is nothing to talk about so much. Other people struggled more than me. Some people work so hard. Of course, I work so hard after the war. Time has changed. America is growing also. They doesn't want the same wrong road. They want right way to treat people.

[After the war] I thought about going back to Japan, but we had two sons and they are pure citizen, see, so we better stay here. I think American try best to do for us. No more always something doing of fright[ening] things or terrible things. I think in many ways very nice the people.

The same persistence has helped recent immigrants from Japan. Tetsuya Matsuura, a top-ranked designer in New York City, told an interviewer of his struggles after arriving in the United States in the early 1980s.

My first weeks in New York I was very discouraged. There was no dormitory at the School of Visual Arts, so I had to stay in a hotel filled with drug addicts and prostitutes. I couldn't believe I'd left a good job in Japan to be in such a situation. I was mugged the second day I was there. I watched TV every night to learn English. I didn't give up. I just watch, watch, watch. I was too proud to quit and go back to Japan.

[After changing jobs several times, Matsuura was hired as a creative director at CBS.] Changing from job to job to get a better position for yourself would be very difficult back in Japan.... I could never have the opportunity to excel personally in Japan like I do here in New York.... There's much more conformity in Japan. If your boss doesn't own his house, you too must rent. If he drives a Toyota, you can't drive a Cadillac. Here you are free to live your life the way you want. My parents have always gotten upset with me because I want to stand out as an individual. They always tell me not to get too much attention, but I want recognition. Here in America, I can be recognized for my own individual merits.

Despite their successes, the older generations of Japanese Americans continued to face questions from their children and grandchildren about internment. As Yoshiko Uchida, who was interned in the Topaz camp, wrote in 1982, many younger Japanese Americans found it hard to understand why their parents and ancestors accepted such treatment without protest.

Today many of the Nisei, having overcome the traumatizing effects of their incarceration and participated in a wide spectrum of American life with no little success, are approaching retirement. Their Sansei children, who experienced the Vietnam War with its violent confrontations and protest marches, have asked questions about those early World War II years.

"Why did you let it happen?" they ask of the evacuation. "Why didn't you fight for your civil rights? Why did you go without a protest to the concentration camps?"

The 88th birthday celebration of Hichiroka John Nozawa. In Japanese tradition, this is a special birthday, when a person gains the right to wear a crimson cap, which signifies that he has begun his second childhood. Eighty-eight origami (folded paper) cranes are made by the guests to celebrate the occasion. The cranes signify long life, happiness, and good luck.

Three young Sansei at a Chicago Cubs baseball game.

Cynthia Kadohata

In 1989, Cynthia Kadohata's first novel, *The Floating World*, received rave reviews and became a best-seller. Kodahata was acclaimed as one of the most talented young Japanese American writers.

Kadohata, however, has mixed feelings about being stereotyped as an "ethnic" writer. She told an interviewer, "When I want to be an Asian writer, then I am one, but I don't like people saying you have to be an Asian writer, and if you do something different, then you're a banana or whatever." (*Banana* is a derogatory term for an Asian who imitates Caucasians—yellow on the outside, white on the inside.)

The Floating World is about a Japanese American family in the post–World War II years. Seen through the eyes of 12-year-old Olivia, the family travels from place to place in search of work. In some respects, the novel reflects Kadohata's own childhood. Her parents were immigrants who spent time in the internment camps, though Kadohata herself was not born until the 1950s. (She refuses to give the exact year of her birth.)

After graduating from the University of Southern California, Kadohata decided to be a writer. She told an editor, "I want to get better, faster." He urged her to enroll in a college workshop for writers. She was not entirely satisfied with the advice she got there. One teacher told her that her "characters were not acting Japanese enough, and I didn't know what that meant, eating sushi or something?"

Kadohata's second novel, *In the Heart of the Valley of Love*, is set in 21st-century Los Angeles, when nonwhites outnumber whites. Though the main character is a young woman of Japanese and African descent, her experiences have little to do with her race. Kadohata insists that her works reflect her own point of view: "I wrote the book, and I'm Asian, and I'm the only person who could have written it."

They were right to ask these questions, for they made us search for some obscured truths and come to a better understanding of ourselves and those times. They are the generation for whom civil rights meant more than just words. They are the generation who taught us to celebrate our ethnicity and discover our ethnic pride. Their compassion and concern for the aging Issei resulted in many worthwhile programs for all Japanese Americans.

It is my generation, however, who lived throught the evacuation of 1942. We are the link to the past and we must provide them with the cultural memory they lack. We must tell them all we can remember, so they can better understand the history of their own people. As they listen to our voices from the past, however, I ask that they remember they are listening in a totally different time; in a totally changed world.

In 1942 the word "ethnic" was yet unknown and ethnic consciousness not yet awakened. There had been no freedom marches, and the voice of Martin Luther King had not been heard. The majority of the American people, supporting their country in a way they considered just, refused to acknowledge the fact that their country was denying the civil rights of fellow Americans. They would not have supported any resistance to our forced removal had it arisen, and indeed such resistance might well have been met with violence as treasonous....

Today I would not allow my civil rights to be denied without strong protest, and I believe there would be many other Americans willing to stand beside me in protest.

As Seichi Hayashida, who had been interned with his wife in Tule Lake and Minidoka, told an interviewer, few people outside the Japanese American community were aware of the camps.

I found out there is so many people, the public in Idaho and the rest of the country, except for the three west coast states, know very little about the experience that we went through. And so in order to educate the people and public...[we wanted to] tell them about our experiences so that it wouldn't happen again. We hope it won't happen again, it should never happen again under the circumstances that we, we went through.

[It was difficult for the Hayashidas even to tell their son.] Well his reaction is that he don't understand how it could have happened...when he was 14 we thought he was old enough to understand if we told him of our experiences, which we did. And first thing he said, "I can't believe that it, it ever happened, should have happened." We explained why and we have given him all the books that related to it, you know, the reasons that led up to it. And he doesn't talk about it, but he knows, I think he probably knows. Both of us told him and explained to him much better than most parents of our age have explained to them, taken the time to.

In 1972, Jeanne Wakatsuki returned to Manzanar, the camp where she and her family had been interned.

I had nearly outgrown the shame and the guilt and the sense of unworthiness. This visit, this pilgrimage, made comprehensible, finally, the traces that remained and would always remain, like a needle. That hollow ache I had carried during the early months of internment had shrunk over the years to a tiny sliver of suspicion about the very person I was. It had grown so small I'd forget it was there. Months might pass before something would remind me. When I first read, in the summer of 1972, about the pressure Japan's economy was putting on American business and how a union in New York City had printed up posters of an American flag with a MADE IN JAPAN written across it, then that needle began to jab. I heard Mama's soft voice from 1945 say, "It's all starting over." I knew it wouldn't. Yet neither would I have been surprised to find the FBI at my door again. I would resist it much more than my parents did, but deep within me something had been prepared for that. Manzanar would always live in my nervous system, a needle with Mama's voice.

For many Japanese Americans, the redress movement was a chance to exorcise the memories of the horrible experience. Mary Sakaguchi Oda spoke to the congressional committee that investigated the internment in 1981.

The most difficult problem for me to overcome as a result of the evacuation was the anger and bitterness which has gradually surfaced over the past 39 years. When the photographs of camp were shown at the Pasadena Art Museum some years ago, I burst into tears and could not stop the tears from flowing. All the pent-up emotion held back for so many years was released. The numbness of the evacuation was finally lifted, and because of the humiliation and shame, I could never tell my four children my true feelings about that event in 1942. I did not want my children to feel the burden of shame and feeling of rejection by their fellow Americans. I wanted them to feel that in spite of what was done to us, this was still the best place in the world to live.

Yuri Kochiyama, who spent the war years in the Jerome, Arkansas, relocation center, expressed her feelings about the redress movement.

Most Japanese Americans who worked years and years for redress never thought it would happen the way it did. The papers have been signed, we will be given reparation, and there was an apology from the government. I think the redress movement itself was very good because it was a learning experience for the Japanese people; we could get out into our communities and speak about what happened to us and link it with experiences of other people.... It showed us, too, how vulnerable everybody is. It showed us that even though there is a constitution, that constitutional rights could be taken away very easily.

A member of the JACL helps a woman fill out the application papers for obtaining redress payments from the U.S. government.

THE WHITE HOUSE
WASHINGTON

A monetary sum and words alone cannot restore lost years or erase painful memories; neither can they fully convey our Nation's resolve to rectify injustice and to uphold the rights of individuals. We can never fully right the wrongs of the past. But we can take a clear stand for justice and recognize that serious injustices were done to Japanese Americans during World War II.

In enacting a law calling for restitution and offering a sincere apology, your fellow Americans have, in a very real sense, renewed their traditional commitment to the ideals of freedom, equality, and justice. You and your family have our best wishes for the future.

Sincerely,

G Bush

A letter signed by President George Bush accompanied each redress check sent to Japanese Americans who were interned during World War II.

Traditional Japanese art has influenced design and art in the United States. Here, a Japanese American in New York creates his own versions of ukiyo-e—prints that were produced in Japan from the 17th to the 19th century. The name refers to the "floating world" of courtesans and actors, who were depicted in the prints.

At an exhibition of Japanese arts and crafts in Seabrook, New Jersey, two kimono-clad women admire an ikebana, or flower arrangement. As with other Japanese arts, ikebana does not overwhelm the viewer with showy displays. A few branches, leaves, or flowers are artfully placed to suggest the beauty and harmony of the natural world.

PRESERVING THE TRADITION

George Sakamoto, who spent part of World War II in internment camps, relocated to Seabrook, New Jersey. In the 1980s, he spoke about ethnic awareness within the Japanese American community.

None of the Sakamotos ever went back to Japan. I don't have the desire to go back. I know no one there. Our parents didn't say much about Japan and Japanese culture. Celebrating these things wasn't too popular when I was growing up—Japanese New Year's, maybe, but not too much—because we were more or less outsiders in California. People tended to say that we were clannish, or that we were different; things like that. So showing an interest in Japanese traditions wasn't too popular.

Today I think people realize the importance of ethnic culture. Ethnic groups show more interest and more pride in their old customs than they did forty or fifty years ago.

Japanese in Japan and the United States celebrate a Girl's Day and a Boy's Day. Yoshiko Uchida remembered the importance of Girl's Day in her childhood and related how she maintains some of the traditions today.

There were certain Japanese customs that we observed regularly. Every year before March 3 [Girl's Day, also called Doll's Festival Day], my mother, sister, and I would open the big brown trunk that had come with Mama from Japan. From its depths we would extract dozens and dozens of small wooden boxes containing the tiny ornamental dolls she had collected over the years. They were not the usual formal set of Imperial Court dolls normally displayed for this festival, but to me they were much more appealing.

My mother's vast and rambling collection included rural folk toys and charms, dolls of eggshell and corn husks, dolls representing famous Noh or Kabuki dances or characters in the folktales she had read to us, miniature dishes and kitchen utensils, and even some of the dolls she had played with as a child herself. It took well over an hour for us to open the boxes and put the collection out for display, but to Mama each doll was like an old friend....

Now it is I who find pleasure in getting the dolls out once a year from their small boxes of paulownia wood. But it is not so much in remembrance of Dolls Festival Day that I display them as in remembrance of my mother and her Japanese ways.

I also remember my parents on the anniversary of their death by placing flowers beside their photograph, just as I had seen them do, perpetuating a Buddhist tradition that had been an intrinsic part of their early lives. The Issei were very close to their dead and their funerals were elaborate and lengthy affairs often attended by hundreds of people. In the early years, these funerals were held at night to accommodate those who worked and couldn't take time off during the day, but even today many of my Nisei friends, following the tradition of their parents, still hold funeral services at night and perpetuate the custom of giving *okoden* (monetary gifts) to the family of the deceased. Our parents' Japaneseness is still very much a part of us.

June Kuramoto, a postwar immigrant who formed the musical group Hiroshima with her brother and friends, remembered her first exposure to Japanese music.

When I was very young, my mother took me to see Madame Kazue Kudo performing in a koto [Japanese stringed instrument] concert. I instantly fell in love with the harplike sound of this beautiful Japanese musical instrument. I begged my mother to ask Madame Kudo to teach me how to play the koto. My mother was shocked that this little kid would be asking to play such an instrument. Madame Kudo became my teacher and ever since then I have been studying the koto with her. Through the years, the koto has become a link between my two countries: Japan and America.

Osuke Takizawa, born in 1886 in Nagano prefecture, emigrated to the United States as a young man. He was interviewed when he was 88 years old.

I believe children and grandchildren must know the way their grandparents walked. The Sansei and the Yonsei should know their grandparents' history. One thing for sure is that the Issei in the United States were all diligent and did their best. All of the Issei wish that the Sansei and the Yonsei learn and appreciate our history. That is greater filial piety than building a large monument or holding a special celebration for us.

You are a homeless dog without your identity. Though we are U.S. citizens, we are Japanese. The color of our faces and so on.... Losing identity is the same as losing money; you lose your way of life.

Jane Muramoto Yung, a Sansei, spoke to an interviewer in 1989 about the effect that prejudice had on ethnic pride.

As for customs and practices, New Years has always been big for me, more so than Christmas. It's a time when I feel very Japanese. As a kid we'd always go to Bachan's [Grandma's] for family and Japanese "soul food." Now we always go to my folks. We didn't celebrate other Japanese holidays or speak Japanese because my grandparents died early. I know the camp experience made my folks minimize Japanese customs in our house. My dad told us we probably would have gone to Japanese school to speak Japanese if it

Ellison S. Onizuka

On January 24, 1985, the space shuttle *Discovery* roared into orbit. One of its five crew members was Ellison S. Onizuka, who that day became the first Asian American to travel in space. Onizuka took along a packet of mementoes—Kona coffee from his birthplace, Hawaii; a Buddhist medallion that had been a gift from his father; and uniform patches from the all-Nisei 442nd Combat Team.

Onizuka recalled that on the flight, "I looked down as we passed over Hawaii and thought about all the sacrifices of all the people who helped me along the way. My grandparents, who were contract laborers; my parents, who did without to send me to college; my schoolteachers, coaches and ministers—all the past generations who pulled together to create the present."

Onizuka was born in 1946 in Keopu, Hawaii, where his parents owned a store. He became an honor student and joined the 4-H Club, Young Buddhist Association, and the Boy Scouts, reaching the rank of Eagle Scout. He was particularly proud of playing center field on his high school's championship baseball team.

In 1964, Onizuka enrolled in the aeronautical engineering program at the University of Colorado. After graduation, he joined the U.S. Air Force, completing advanced studies in aerospace science. When the National Aeronautics and Space Administration (NASA) took applications for the space shuttle program, Onizuka volunteered. Out of 8,100 candidates, he was one of 35 who were selected to be astronauts.

After his first trip into space, Onizuka was chosen to fly on the *Challenger* mission in January 1986. Tragically, the shuttle exploded 73 seconds after launch, killing everyone on board. Six years earlier, Onizuka had been invited to speak to the graduating class of his old high school. He told them, "Make your life count—and the world will be a better place because you tried."

Dr. William Inouye with a "thousand crane" origami that his sister Dr. Miyoko Inouye Bassett made for him. Origami is the traditional Japanese art of paper folding. Each of the thousand cranes was made from a single sheet of paper.

Members of the Nakai family make rice cakes, a Japanese custom for the New Year's celebration.

weren't for camp. It got ingrained in them to raise their children 100% Americans.

Kelly Hanzawa was born in Bridgeton, New Jersey. Her parents spent the years of World War II in an internment camp, leaving to work at Seabrook after the war. She described some of her family's New Year's traditions.

The family gets together and has a traditional breakfast. Then the female members of the family stay home and receive gifts from people who visit. My father was always gone with the men, going from house to house to wish the families Happy New Year's.

It is a big holiday for Japanese families. Food is prepared for days on end—mochi, for example. For breakfast we would have ozoni, which is fish broth made with rice cakes. Also a lot of liquor is served. And I still observe this tradition.

Kesaya E. Noda, a Sansei living in California, wrote about her complicated feelings of ethnic and personal identity.

The voice in me remembers that I am always a *Japanese American* in the eyes of many. A third-generation German American is an American. A third-generation Japanese American is a Japanese American. Being Japanese means being a danger to the country during the war and knowing how to use chopsticks. I wear this history on my face.

I move to the other side. I see a different light and claim a different context. My race is a line that stretches across ocean and time to link me to the shrine where my grandmother was raised. Two high, white banners lift in the wind at the top of the stone steps leading to the shrine. It is time for the summer festival. Black characters are written against the sky as boldly as the clouds, as lightly as kites, as sharply as the big black crows I used to see above the fields in New Hampshire. At festival time there is liquor and food, ritual, discipline, and abandonment. There is music and drunkenness and invocation. There is hope. Another season has come. Another season has gone.

I am racially Japanese. I have a certain claim to this crazy place where the prayers intoned by a neighboring Shinto priest (standing in for my grandmother's nephew who is sick) are drowned out by the rehearsals for the pop singing contest in which most of the villagers will compete later that night. The village elders, the priest, and I stand respectfully upon the immaculate, shining wooden floor of the outer shrine, bowing our heads before the hidden powers. During the patchy intervals when I can hear him, I notice the priest has a stutter. His voice flutters up to my ears only occasionally because two men and a woman are singing gustily into a microphone in the compoud, testing the sound system.... Rock music and Shinto prayers.

This man practices the art of calligraphy, or beautiful handwriting. A person's writing style is supposed to be an indication of his character.

Students display their work at the Japanese Weekend School of New Jersey, in Englewood Cliffs. Many Japanese American children attend such schools to learn the Japanese language and culture. These schools also offer extra work in regular school subjects, sports programs, and classes in arts and crafts.

These Chicago children are dressed in samurai costumes. The samurai, who combined martial arts skills with a strong sensitivity to beauty, continue to symbolize Japanese culture.

Mizue Sawano is an artist who lives and paints in New York City. Nature and its many forms are favorite subjects of Japanese artists.

The wedding picture of Susan Tamura's grandparents, in Oakland, California, before World War I.

Susan Tamura's mother, Kazuko Nozawa, as a baby, with her parents.

THE KAWAICHI AND TAMURA FAMILIES

Ken Kawaichi and Susan Tamura live in Oakland, California. Kawaichi has been a state judge since 1975, and Tamura currently practices estate-planning law. They were married in 1973 and have two children, Kathryn and K. C.

Q: *When did the first members of your family come to the United States?*

Susan Tamura:

My grandfather Tamura came to the West Coast around 1905. That was during the Russian-Japanese War, and I believe he was trying to avoid the military draft. According to my uncle, both my grandfather and Ken's grandfather were farmers in the same area, in Fountain Valley, California. My uncle and Ken's father attended the same high school.

The other grandfather, my mother's father, took a different route. He left Japan with some missionaries and traveled through Asia and Europe, probably entering the United States at New York City, Ellis Island.

Ken Kawaichi:

Both sides of my family were fairly conventional in their arrival. They all came here to California around the turn of the century. However, my mother's father settled in Los Angeles and became a produce broker. He had been one in Japan. He did fairly well here, and he owned one of the first automobiles in Los Angeles. But he lost a lot of money in the stock market crash of 1929.

Q: *Tell us about your parents' experiences.*

Susan Tamura:

My father was a justice of the court of appeals in California. He attended junior college in Santa Ana and Pomona College in Claremont, California. My uncle helped him financially and my father was able to attend Boalt Hall Law School at U.C. Berkeley. He returned to Santa Ana to practice law and he met my mother. My parents were married in 1941, three months before the bombing of Pearl Harbor.

My parents were sent to the Poston I Relocation Camp in Arizona. My mother became pregnant and my parents transferred to the Amache Camp to be near my mother's family. My brother was born, but he died in camp as an infant and he is buried at Amache. He was named Stephen and when my father later chose to adopt an English name, he chose the same name.

One way of getting out of the camps was to agree to move east, so my father enrolled in Harvard Law School as a graduate student. After his graduation he was drafted into the army and was assigned to the all Japanese American 442nd Regiment. As he was shipped out to Europe, the war ended. He spent two years in Italy.

Ken Kawaichi:

My parents were in Poston, too. I was five months old at the time, so I have no personal memories of it. We stayed for about a year and a half, and then my father joined the army. He was a physician. He served in Europe, at first with the 442nd Combat Team, but then was reassigned to a medical unit. After the war, my dad got a job with the Veterans Administration in Wichita, Kansas. That's where I grew up.

Q: Susan, did your family return to the West Coast after the war?

Yes, to Santa Ana, where my father had practiced law. The thing that most impressed me about my father was how much he loved the law. That he continued to trust it, despite what had happened. He and my mother had a bad experience even in Boston, when he was going to law school. The police broke into their apartment, because Massachusetts had an anti-miscegenation law [barring marriages between people of different races]. My parents were both of Japanese descent, but the couple who owned the building were of different races, and the police just broke into my parents' apartment looking for something. It was very impressive to me that my father could have gone through experiences like that, been in a camp, and not be bitter about it.

Q: Did your parents describe to you their experiences in the camps?

Susan Tamura:

Well, we knew about the camps in an odd sense. We would go on Memorial Day to commemorations, and my parents would see other people that they knew. As children, we'd ask, "Well, how do you know this person?" And they would say, "We knew them from the camps." We children didn't quite understand that. We thought, oh, like a summer camp or a church camp.

The older we got, the more questions we asked about the camps. No one wanted to talk about it. I think that the older generations did not want to describe their experiences to us because they were trying to shield and protect us from fear and bitter memories. I think that the people who were angriest about it were those who were young, or teenagers, when they were sent to the camps. They had a real sense of betrayal.

Ken Kawaichi's mother, Margaret, is Nisei Week Queen in Los Angeles in 1938.

Ken Kawaichi's father, George, worked as a physician in Long Beach, California.

Susan Tamura's father, Stephen K. Tamura, reads a newspaper headline declaring the start of World War II.

Susan Tamura's grandfather, Hasamatsu Tamura, founded the Tamura School in Fountain Valley, California. He was one of the pioneers of the area and donated woodworking equipment, a stove, and a sewing machine for the original school.

Ken Kawaichi:

I always thought that the most horrible thing was that they didn't want to say anything about how their rights were violated. They remained publicly silent, but from time to time you could detect the resentment and anger.

Q: Did you experience prejudice while you were growing up?

Susan Tamura:

We experienced the usual name-calling and racial taunts, but we were told by our parents that we could rise above the prejudice and bigotry by working hard at school. In high school, I was part of a very small Japanese American minority. We went to social events that were organized by the JACL youth group. So we had friends at the high school, and Japanese American friends that were part of the church and the JACL.

Q: Like your father, Susan, you went on to become a lawyer yourself. Were you carrying on the family tradition?

To some extent, but that was during the 1960s, and my choosing a legal career was really a product of the times. People felt that the law could make a real difference, and they could change things. I don't know if I would feel that way today. I attended Pomona College, like my father. Ken did too, and now our daughter is there as well.

Q: Did the two of you meet at Pomona?

No, we met at Berkeley, where Ken was a professor of ethnic studies, and I was a law student and a teaching assistant in Asian-American studies. I think the first time I talked to him, I was a young law student working on a volunteer project to arrange bail for prisoners, and consulted him for help.

Q: In raising your children, did you observe any holidays or traditions that reflected your Japanese heritage?

Our son played basketball for the Oakland Buddhist Church. Both children took part in activities there. Our family celebrates New Year's Day in a way that is a hybrid between Japanese and American customs. We have an open house on January 1, not New Year's Eve. When I was growing up, my family gathered at my grandparents' home. My father told me that his family would celebrate New Year's Day, but the women stayed home and cooked while the men went around visiting each other's houses. We don't do it that way. We have it in our home for our relatives and friends. Our celebration differs in some other ways from the one in Japan. People used to give away token money to the children. We don't do that. We also serve different kinds of food. My sister-in-law, for example, is Jewish, so we have some chopped liver and matzos based on her recipe.

Q: Many Japanese Americans are unhappy about being portrayed as the "model minority." How do you feel about this?

Susan Tamura:

I think this arises in part out of the camp experience. People point to Japanese Americans and say, "Look what happened to them, and yet they endured it and prospered." But not all Japanese Americans are doing so well. And even for those who are, great sacrifices were made. Our grandparents could not own land or become citizens. Our parents could not get jobs for which they were qualified.

People came out of the camps with the feeling that they had to do more, to become better, to prove that they were "good Americans." That's what I don't like. I wanted to give my children the feeling that you don't have to achieve more than somebody else to be treated equally.

Ken Kawaichi:

There's another aspect of the camp experience that is involved. Right away, you had the American-born young generation having to take charge. Because they spoke English, they had to answer the questions that the authorities asked at the camps. Those young people had a lot of responsibility at an early age, and afterward there was no way to go back to the social structure that existed before. This put a lot of pressure on that generation to make something out of their lives.

Susan Tamura:

I think it was tragic, too, that those who went into the camps felt that they had to get rid of things before they went in. Everything that was Japanese. In some cases, people destroyed or buried their family pictures and mementoes. One of the things that people like to say about the camp experience was that it was an anomaly, an exception. But it happened in a context. It was part of the climate of racial prejudice that existed before the war. And later, when I was a young person, there was the war in Vietnam, with its underlying racism.

Even today, we see a lot of anti-Asian feelings expressed in the media. The recent passage of Proposition 187 in California [blocking illegal immigrants from receiving social services] is also evidence of today's anti-immigrant spirit.

Recently, Ken and I supported a project to train teachers to include the camp experience in the school curriculum. I think it's a good idea that the schools are now stressing the different backgrounds of the many kinds of people who are Americans. People are starting to realize how much all the immigrant groups had in common.

Ken Kawaichi:

Hopefully, the gains we have made in society by attempting to understand each other and being more sensitive to the needs of other racial and ethnic communities will carry us past current scapegoating to fulfill the promise our grandparents perceived when they came to the United States.

The Tamura family around 1980 at the home of Susan's parents in Santa Ana, California.

Susan Tamura and Ken Kawaichi with their daughter, Katy, and their son, K. C.

JAPANESE AMERICAN TIMELINE

1868

First Japanese laborers, the *gannen-mono*, arrive in Hawaii to work on sugar plantations.

1869

Wakamatsu Colony is founded in California.

1877

Japanese students in San Francisco found the Fukuinkai, or Gospel Society.

1884

Labor recruiters from Hawaiian plantations arrive in Japan. Sponsored by the Japanese government, about 945 contract laborers sail for Hawaii the following year.

1898

First Shinto shrine in Hawaii is built at Hilo.

United States annexes Hawaii; two years later it becomes a territory.

1900

First Uchinanchu, or Okinawans, arrive in Hawaii.

Labor groups in San Francisco organize anti-Japanese protest rally.

1905

San Francisco labor leaders form the Asiatic Exclusion League to demand a halt to Japanese immigration.

1906

San Francisco school board passes a resolution to segregate Asian children from others.

1908

As part of the Gentlemen's Agreement, the Japanese government stops issuing passports to laborers headed for the United States. In return, President Theodore Roosevelt persuades San Francisco school officials to integrate Asian children.

1909

About 7,000 Japanese Hawaiian laborers in the Higher Wage Association go on strike.

1913

California passes the Alien Land Act, making it illegal for Asian immigrants to own land.

1915

Federation of Japanese Labor (FJL) is formed in Hawaii. The following year, it leads a major strike of Japanese Hawaiian plantation workers.

1920

A second Alien Land Act in California bars Issei from leasing or sharecropping land.

1924

Congress passes a comprehensive immigration act that bars further immigration by Japanese.

1925

The Supreme Court's ruling in *Toyota* v. *United States* affirms that Asian immigrants are ineligible to become U.S. citizens. The ruling strips Hidemitsu Toyota of the citizenship granted for his military service during World War I.

1930

First convention of the Japanese American Citizens League (JACL) is held in Seattle.

December 7, 1941

Japanese planes bomb the U.S. naval base at Pearl Harbor, Hawaii. Immediately, FBI agents start to round up Issei leaders of Japanese American communities in Hawaii and the mainland.

February 19, 1942

Executive Order 9066 authorizes the War Department to remove anyone from designated military areas. During the following year, Japanese Americans in parts of California, Oregon, Washington, and Arizona were forced into internment camps in isolated areas. Most remained there until the end of World War II in 1945.

1943

Nisei volunteers and draftees from Hawaii are formed into the 100th Infantry Battalion. Nisei from the mainland begin training as the 442nd Regimental Combat Team. Later, the 100th became part of the 442nd; their members distinguished themselves for bravery in combat in Europe.

1944

U.S. Supreme Court's ruling in *Korematsu* v. *United States* affirms the legality of the forced internment of Japanese Americans.

1952

Congress passes McCarran-Walter Act, which allows Issei to obtain citizenship and authorizes a small number of immigrants from Japan.

1959

Hawaii becomes a state. Daniel K. Inouye is elected the first Japanese American member of Congress.

1965

Congress passes the Immigration and Nationality Act, which sets quotas for Asian immigrants equal to those for Europeans.

1976

The JACL organizes the National Committee for Redress to study the issue of obtaining proper compensation for those detained in camps during World War II.

1988

Congress provides for payments of $20,000 to each surviving internee from the internment camps. Payments began in 1990.

FURTHER READING

General Accounts of Japanese American History

Hazama, Dorothy Ochiai, and Jane Okamoto Komeiji. *Okage Sama De: The Japanese in Hawai'i, 1885–1985.* Honolulu: Bess Press, 1986.

Hosokawa, Bill. *Nisei: The Quiet Americans.* Niwot: University Press of Colorado, 1992.

Ichioka, Yuji. *The Issei: The World of the First Generation Japanese Immigrants.* New York: Free Press, 1988.

Kikumura, Akemi. *Issei Pioneers: Hawaii and the Mainland, 1885–1924.* Los Angeles: Japanese American National Museum, 1992.

Niiya, Brian, ed. *Japanese American History.* New York: Facts on File, 1993.

O'Brien, David J., and Stephen S. Fugita. *The Japanese American Experience.* Bloomington: Indiana University Press, 1991.

Odo, Franklin, and Kazuko Sinoto. *A Pictorial History of the Japanese in Hawai'i, 1885–1924.* Honolulu: Bishop Museum Press, 1985.

Specific Aspects of Japanese American History

Ethnic Studies Oral History Project, United Okinawan Association of Hawaii. *Uchinanchu: A History of Okinawans in Hawaii.* Honolulu: Ethnic Studies Program, University of Hawaii at Manoa, 1981.

Hatamiya, Leslie T. *Righting a Wrong: Japanese Americans and the Passage of the Civil Liberties Act of 1988.* Stanford, Calif.: Stanford University Press, 1993.

Kimura, Yukiko. *Issei: Japanese Immigrants in Hawaii.* Honolulu: University of Hawaii Press, 1988.

Lukes, Timothy J., and Gary Y. Okihiro. *Japanese Legacy: Farming and Community Life in California's Santa Clara Valley.* Cupertino: California History Center, 1985.

Murase, Ichiro Mike. *Little Tokyo: One Hundred Years in Pictures.* Los Angeles: Visual Communications/Asian American Studies Central, 1983.

Nakano, Mei T. *Japanese American Women: Three Generations, 1890–1990.* Berkeley, Calif.: Mina Press, 1990.

Saiki, Patsy Sumie. *Japanese Women in Hawaii: The First 100 Years.* Honolulu: Kisaku, 1985.

Walls, Thomas K. *The Japanese Texans.* San Antonio: Institute of Texan Cultures, 1987.

Weglyn, Michi. *Years of Infamy: The Untold Story of America's Concentration Camps.* New York: Morrow, 1978.

First-Person Accounts of Japanese American Life

Glenn, Evelyn Nakano. *Issei, Nisei, War Bride.* Philadelphia: Temple University Press, 1986.

Ito, Kazuo. *Issei: A History of Japanese Immigrants in North America.* Translated by Shinichiro Nakamura and Jean S. Gerard. Seattle: Japanese Community Service, 1973.

Kikuchi, Charles. *The Kikuchi Diary.* Edited by John Modell. Urbana: University of Illinois Press, 1973.

Kikumura, Akemi. *Through Harsh Winters: The Life of a Japanese Immigrant Woman.* Novato, Calif.: Chandler & Sharp, 1981.

Kodama-Nishimoto, Michi, Warren S. Nishimoto, and Cynthia A. Oshiro. *Hanahana: An Oral History Anthology of Hawaii's Working People.* Honolulu: Ethnic Studies Oral History Project, University of Hawaii at Manoa, 1984.

Matsumoto, David Mas. *Country Voices: The Oral History of a Japanese American Family Farm Community.* Del Rey, Calif.: Inaka Countryside Publications, 1987.

Mura, David. *Turning Japanese: Memoirs of a Sansei.* New York: Atlantic Monthly Press, 1991.

Sarasohn, Eileen Sunada. *The Issei: Portrait of a Pioneer.* Palo Alto, Calif.: Pacific Books, 1983.

Sone, Monica. *Nisei Daughter.* Seattle: University of Washington Press, 1953.

Uchida, Yoshiko. *Desert Exile: The Uprooting of a Japanese American Family.* Seattle: University of Washington Press, 1982.

Wakatsuki, Jeanne. *Farewell to Manzanar.* Boston: Houghton Mifflin, 1973.

Stories, Novels, and Poems by Japanese Americans

Asian Women United of California, ed. *Making Waves: An Anthology of Writings by and about Asian American Women.* Boston: Beacon Press, 1989.

Inada, Lawson F. *Before the War: Poems as They Happened.* New York: Morrow, 1971.

Kadohata, Cynthia. *The Floating World.* New York: Viking, 1989.

Kanazawa, Tooru J. *Sushi and Sourdough: A Novel.* Seattle: University of Washington Press, 1989.

Mirikitani, Janice, et al., eds. *Ayumi: A Japanese American Anthology.* San Francisco: Japanese American Anthology Committee, 1980.

Miyamoto, Kazuo. *Hawaii: End of the Rainbow.* Tokyo: Charles E. Tuttle, 1964.

Okada, John. *No-No Boy.* 1957. Reprint. Seattle: University of Washington Press, 1979.

TEXT CREDITS

Main Text

p. 12: Toru Matsumoto and Marion Olive Lerrigo, *A Brother Is a Stranger* (New York: John Day, 1946), 2-3.

p. 13, top: Matsumoto and Lerrigo, *A Brother Is a Stranger,* 2.

p. 13, bottom: Kihachi Hirakawa, *Autobiography* (Seattle: University of Washington Manuscripts and Archives, Accession Number 2418), 1-4.

p. 14: *Hanahana: An Oral History Anthology of Hawaii's Working People,* by Michi Kodama-Nishimoto, Warren S. Nishimoto, and Cynthia A. Oshiro. Published by the Ethnic Studies Oral History Project (renamed the Center for Oral History in 1987), University of Hawaii at Manoa, Honolulu, 1984. Pp.148-50.

p. 15: *Uchinanchu: A History of Okinawans in Hawaii.* Edited by Michi Kodama-Nishimoto and Mitsugu Sakihara. Published by Ethnic Studies Oral History Project (renamed the Center for Oral History in 1987), University of Hawaii at Manoa and the United Okinawan Association of Hawaii, Honolulu, 1981. Pp. 491-92.

p. 16, top: From *The Issei: Portrait of a Pioneer,* edited by Eileen Sunada Sarasohn. Copyright © 1983 by the Issei Oral History Project, Inc. Pacific Books, Publishers, Palo Alto, Calif. Pp. 30-31.

p. 16, bottom: Reprinted by permission of the publisher from *Through Harsh Winters: The Life of a Japanese Immigrant Woman,* by Akemi Kikumura. Copyright © 1981 by Chandler & Sharp Publishers, Inc., Novato, Calif. All rights reserved. Pages 17-18.

p. 17: From *The Issei: Portrait of a Pioneer,* edited by Eileen Sunada Sarasohn. Copyright © 1983 by the Issei Oral History Project, Inc. Pacific Books, Publishers, Palo Alto, Calif. Pp. 36-37.

p. 18: From *The Issei: Portrait of a Pioneer,* edited by Eileen Sunada Sarasohn. Copyright © 1983 by the Issei Oral History Project, Inc. Pacific Books, Publishers, Palo Alto, Calif. Pp. 26-27.

p. 19, top: From *The Issei: Portrait of a Pioneer,* edited by Eileen Sunada Sarasohn. Copyright © 1983 by the Issei Oral History Project, Inc. Pacific Books, Publishers, Palo Alto, Calif. Page 23.

p. 19, bottom: From *The Issei: Portrait of a Pioneer,* edited by Eileen Sunada Sarasohn. Copyright © 1983 by the Issei Oral History Project, Inc. Pacific Books, Publishers, Palo Alto, Calif. Pp. 24-25.

p. 20, top: *Oral History Recorder,* newsletter of the Oral History Project (renamed Center for Oral History in 1987), Social Science Research Institute, University of Hawaii at Manoa, vol. 2, no. 1 (Winter 1985). Page 3.

p. 20, bottom: Hamilton Holt, ed., *The Life Stories of Undistinguished Americans As Told by Themselves* (New York: Routledge, 1990), 159.

p. 21, top: Kazuo Ito, *Issei: A History of Japanese Immigrants in North America,* trans. Shinichiro Nakamura and Jean S. Gerard (Seattle: Japanese Community Service, 1973), 35.

p. 21, middle: Reprinted by permission of the publisher from *Through Harsh Winters: The Life of a Japanese Immigrant Woman,* by Akemi Kikumura. Copyright © 1981 by Chandler & Sharp Publishers, Inc., Novato, Calif. All rights reserved. Page 25.

p. 21, bottom: June Namias, *First Generation* (Boston: Beacon Press, 1978), 75.

p. 24, top: From *The Issei: Portrait of a Pioneer,* edited by Eileen Sunada Sarasohn. Copyright © 1983 by the Issei Oral History Project, Inc. Pacific Books, Publishers, Palo Alto, Calif. Page 37.

p. 24, middle: Ito, *Issei,* 28.

p. 24, bottom: From *The Issei: Portrait of a Pioneer,* edited by Eileen Sunada Sarasohn. Copyright © 1983 by the Issei Oral History Project, Inc. Pacific Books, Publishers, Palo Alto, Calif. Pp. 33-34.

p. 25, top: Ronald Takaki, *A Different Mirror* (Boston: Little, Brown, 1993) 39.

p. 25, middle: *Uchinanchu: A History of Okinawans in Hawaii.* Edited by Michi Kodama-Nishimoto and Mitsugu Sakihara. Published by Ethnic Studies Oral History Project (renamed the Center for Oral History in 1987), University of Hawaii at Manoa and the United Okinawan Association of Hawaii, Honolulu, 1981. Pp. 403-4.

p. 25, bottom: Hirakawa, *Autobiography,* 13-14.

p. 26, top: *Oral History Recorder,* newsletter of the Oral History Project (renamed Center for Oral History in 1987), Social Science Research Institute, University of Hawaii at Manoa, vol. 2, no. 1 (Winter 1985). Page 3.

p. 26, bottom: Ito, *Issei,* 12-13.

p. 27, top: *Uchinanchu: A History of Okinawans in Hawaii.* Edited by Michi Kodama-Nishimoto and Mitsugu Sakihara. Published by Ethnic Studies Oral History Project (renamed the Center for Oral History in 1987), University of Hawaii at Manoa and the United Okinawan Association of Hawaii, Honolulu, 1981. Page 379.

p. 27, bottom: *Hanahana: An Oral History Anthology of Hawaii's Working People,* by Michi Kodama-Nishimoto, Warren S. Nishimoto, and Cynthia A. Oshiro. Published by the Ethnic Studies Oral History Project (renamed the Center for Oral History in 1987), University of Hawaii at Manoa, Honolulu, 1984. Page 153.

p. 28, top: Bill Hosokawa, *Nisei: The Quiet Americans* (Niwot, Colo.: University Press of Colorado, 1992), 48.

p. 28, bottom: Ito, *Issei,* 32.

p. 29, top: Ito, *Issei,* 39.

p. 29, middle: Ito, *Issei,* 40.

p. 29, bottom: From *The Issei: Portrait of a Pioneer,* edited by Eileen Sunada Sarasohn. Copyright © 1983 by the Issei Oral History Project, Inc. Pacific Books, Publishers, Palo Alto, Calif. Pp. 53-54.

p. 30, top: *Uchinanchu: A History of Okinawans in Hawaii.* Edited by Michi Kodama-Nishimoto and Mitsugu Sakihara. Published by Ethnic Studies Oral History Project (renamed the Center for Oral History in 1987), University of Hawaii at Manoa and the United Okinawan Association of Hawaii, Honolulu, 1981. Pp. 379-80.

p. 30, bottom: From *The Issei: Portrait of a Pioneer,* edited by Eileen Sunada Sarasohn. Copyright © 1983 by the Issei Oral History Project, Inc. Pacific Books, Publishers, Palo Alto, Calif. Page 50.

p. 31: *Uchinanchu: A History of Okinawans in Hawaii.* Edited by Michi Kodama-Nishimoto and Mitsugu Sakihara. Published by Ethnic Studies Oral History Project (renamed the Center for Oral History in 1987), University of Hawaii at Manoa and the United Okinawan Association of Hawaii, Honolulu, 1981. Pp. 404-5.

p. 36, top: *Oral History Recorder,* newsletter of the Oral History Project (renamed Center for Oral History in 1987), Social Science Research Institute, University of Hawaii at Manoa, vol. 2, no. 1 (Winter 1985). Page 3.

p. 36, middle: From *The Issei: Portrait of a Pioneer,* edited by Eileen Sunada Sarasohn. Copyright © 1983 by the Issei Oral History Project, Inc. Pacific Books, Publishers, Palo Alto, Calif. Pp. 49-50.

p. 36, bottom: From *The Issei: Portrait of a Pioneer,* edited by Eileen Sunada Sarasohn. Copyright © 1983 by the Issei Oral History Project, Inc. Pacific Books, Publishers, Palo Alto, Calif. Page 50.

p. 37: Ito, *Issei,* 56-57.

p. 38, top: Dorothy Ochiai Hazama and Jane Okamoto Komeiji, *Okage Sama De: The Japanese in Hawai'i, 1885-1985* (Honolulu: Bess Press, 1986), 63-64.

p. 38, bottom: *Uchinanchu: A History of Okinawans in Hawaii.* Edited by Michi Kodama-Nishimoto and Mitsugu Sakihara. Published by Ethnic Studies Oral History Project (renamed the Center for Oral History in 1987), University of Hawaii at Manoa and the United Okinawan Association of Hawaii, Honolulu, 1981. Pp. 488-89.

p. 39, top: Ito, *Issei,* 192.

p. 39, bottom: Patsy Sumie Saiki, *Japanese Women in Hawaii: The First 100 Years* (Honolulu: Kisaku, 1985), 67.

p. 40: Ito, *Issei,* 249.

p. 41, top: From *The Issei: Portrait of a Pioneer,* edited by Eileen Sunada Sarasohn. Copyright © 1983 by the Issei Oral History Project, Inc. Pacific Books, Publishers, Palo Alto, Calif. Page 55.

p. 41, middle: From *The Issei: Portrait of a Pioneer,* edited by Eileen Sunada Sarasohn. Copyright © 1983 by the Issei Oral History Project, Inc. Pacific Books, Publishers, Palo Alto, Calif. Page 52.

p. 41, bottom: From *The Issei: Portrait of a Pioneer,* edited by Eileen Sunada Sarasohn. Copyright © 1983 by the Issei Oral History Project, Inc. Pacific Books, Publishers, Palo Alto, Calif. Page 59.

p. 42, top: Reprinted by permission of the publisher from *Through Harsh Winters: The Life of a Japanese Immigrant Woman,* by Akemi Kikumura. Copyright © 1981 by Chandler & Sharp Publishers, Inc., Novato, Calif. All rights reserved. Page 28.

p. 42, bottom: *Hanahana: An Oral History Anthology of Hawaii's Working People,* by Michi Kodama-Nishimoto, Warren S. Nishimoto, and Cynthia A. Oshiro. Published by the Ethnic Studies Oral History Project (renamed the Center for Oral History in 1987), University of Hawaii at Manoa, Honolulu, 1984. Page 156.

p. 43: Matsumoto and Lerrigo, *A Brother Is a Stranger,* 120-21, 135.

p. 48: *Oral History Recorder,* newsletter of the Oral History Project (renamed Center for Oral History in 1987), Social Science Research Institute, University of Hawaii at Manoa, vol. 2, no. 1 (Winter 1985). Pp. 3-4.

p. 49: *Uchinanchu: A History of Okinawans in Hawaii.* Edited by Michi Kodama-Nishimoto and Mitsugu Sakihara. Published by Ethnic Studies Oral History Project (renamed the Center for Oral History in 1987), University of Hawaii at Manoa and the United Okinawan Association of Hawaii, Honolulu, 1981. Pp. 360-61.

p. 50: *Uchinanchu: A History of Okinawans in Hawaii.* Edited by Michi Kodama-Nishimoto and Mitsugu Sakihara. Published by Ethnic Studies Oral History Project (renamed the Center for Oral History in 1987), University of Hawaii at Manoa and the United Okinawan Association of Hawaii, Honolulu, 1981. Pp. 54-55.

p. 51: Hazama and Komeiji, *Okage Sama De,* 34.

p. 52, top: Hazama and Komeiji, *Okage Sama De,* 34-35.

p. 52, middle: Saiki, *Japanese Women in Hawaii,* 68-69.

p. 52, bottom: Hazama and Komeiji, *Okage Sama De,* 55.

p. 53: *Hanahana: An Oral History Anthology of Hawaii's Working People,* by Michi Kodama-Nishimoto, Warren S. Nishimoto, and Cynthia A. Oshiro. Published by the Ethnic Studies Oral History Project (renamed the Center for Oral History in 1987), University of Hawaii at Manoa, Honolulu, 1984. Pp. 158-59.

p. 54, top: Saiki, *Japanese Women In Hawaii,* 70-71.

p. 54, bottom: *Uchinanchu: A History of Okinawans in Hawaii.* Edited by Michi Kodama-Nishimoto and Mitsugu Sakihara. Published by Ethnic Studies Oral History Project (renamed the Center for Oral History in 1987), University of Hawaii at Manoa and the United Okinawan Association of Hawaii, Honolulu, 1981. Pp. 386-87.

p. 55, top: *Hanahana: An Oral History Anthology of Hawaii's Working People,* by Michi Kodama-Nishimoto, Warren S. Nishimoto, and Cynthia A. Oshiro. Published by the Ethnic Studies Oral History Project (renamed the Center for Oral History in 1987), University of Hawaii at Manoa, Honolulu, 1984. Pp. 159-61.

p. 55, bottom: *Hanahana: An Oral History Anthology of Hawaii's Working People,* by Michi Kodama-Nishimoto, Warren S. Nishimoto, and Cynthia A. Oshiro. Published by the Ethnic Studies Oral History Project (renamed the Center for Oral History in 1987), University of Hawaii at Manoa, Honolulu, 1984. Pp. 64-65.

p. 56, top: Holt, *Life Stories,* 161.

p. 56, bottom: Yuji Ichioka, *The Issei: The World of the First Generation Japanese Immigrants, 1885–1924* (New York: The Free Press, 1988), 25-26.

p. 57, top: Ichioka, *The Issei,* 22.

p. 57, bottom: Ichioka, *The Issei,* 21.

p. 58: Ito, *Issei,* 310.

p. 59, top: Ito, *Issei,* 410-11.

p. 59, bottom: Tsurutani Hisashi, *America-Bound: The Japanese and the Opening of the American West* (Tokyo: The Japan Times, 1989), 152-55.

p. 60: Ito, *Issei,* 575-76.

p. 61: From *The Issei: Portrait of a Pioneer,* edited by Eileen Sunada Sarasohn. Copyright © 1983 by the Issei Oral History Project, Inc. Pacific Books, Publishers, Palo Alto, Calif. Pp. 92-93.

p. 62: Ito, *Issei,* 357-61.

p. 63, top: Hisashi, *America-Bound,* 165-66.

p. 63, bottom: Ito, *Issei,* 258-59.

p. 64: Ito, *Issei,* 472-73.

p. 65: Reprinted by permission of the publisher from *Through Harsh Winters: The Life of a Japanese Immigrant Woman,* by Akemi Kikumura. Copyright © 1981 by Chandler & Sharp Publishers, Inc., Novato, Calif. All rights reserved. Pages 30-32.

p. 66: Hosokawa, *Nisei,* 70.

p. 67, top: Timothy J. Lukes and Gary Y. Okihiro, *Japanese Legacy: Farmer and Community Life in California's Santa Clara Valley* (Cupertino: California History Center, 1985), 60.

p. 67, bottom: Asada, Itsuko (Iddy), *Oral Histories of Seabrook Residents: The History of the Taniguchi Family* (Greenwich, N.J.: Cumberland County Historical Society, 1986), 5.

p. 68, top: Lukes and Okihiro, *Japanese Legacy,* 70-72.

p. 68, bottom: Lukes and Okihiro, *Japanese Legacy,* 59.

p. 69: From *The Issei: Portrait of a Pioneer,* edited by Eileen Sunada Sarasohn. Copyright © 1983 by the Issei Oral History Project, Inc. Pacific Books, Publishers, Palo Alto, Calif. Pp. 86-87.

p. 70, top: Ito, *Issei,* 95.

p. 70, middle: From *The Issei: Portrait of a Pioneer,* edited by Eileen Sunada Sarasohn. Copyright © 1983 by the Issei Oral History Project, Inc. Pacific Books, Publishers, Palo Alto, Calif. Pp. 60.

p. 70, bottom: Salvatore J. LaGumina and Frank J. Cavaioli, *The Ethnic Dimension in American Society* (Boston: Holbrook Press, 1974), 107-8.

p. 71, top: Howard L. Green and Lee R. Parks, *What Is Ethnicity?* (Trenton: New Jersey Historical Commission, 1987), 16.

p. 71, bottom: Yoshiko Uchida, *Desert Exile: The Uprooting of a Japanese American Family* (Seattle: University of Washington Press, 1982), 41-42.

p. 76, top: Ichioka, *The Issei,* 23.

p. 76, middle: Lukes and Okihiro, *Japanese Legacy,* 24.

p. 76, bottom: Hosokawa, *Nisei,* 164-66.

p. 77: Namias, *First Generation,* 130.

p. 78, top: Valerie J. Matsumoto, *Farming the Home Place* (Ithaca, N.Y.: Cornell University Press, 1993), 175.

p. 78, bottom: *Uchinanchu: A History of Okinawans in Hawaii.* Edited by Michi Kodama-Nishimoto and Mitsugu Sakihara. Published by Ethnic Studies Oral History Project (renamed the Center for Oral History in 1987), University of Hawaii at Manoa and the United Okinawan Association of Hawaii, Honolulu, 1981. Page 374.

p. 79, top: *Hanahana: An Oral History Anthology of Hawaii's Working People,* by Michi Kodama-Nishimoto, Warren S. Nishimoto, and Cynthia A. Oshiro. Published by the Ethnic Studies Oral History Project (renamed the Center for Oral History in 1987), University of Hawaii at Manoa, Honolulu, 1984. Pp. 61-62.

p. 79, bottom: Excerpts from pp. 9-10 of *Farewell to Manzanar* by James D. and Jeanne Wakatsuki Houston. Copyright © 1973 by James D. Houston. Reprinted by permission of Houghton Mifflin Co. All rights reserved.

p. 80, top: David Mas Matsumoto, *Country Voices: The Oral History of a Japanese Community* (Del Rey, Calif.: Inaka Countryside Publications, 1985), 36.

p. 80, middle: Ito, *Issei,* 835.

p. 80, bottom: From *Nisei Daughter* by Monica Sone. Copyright © 1953 by Monica Sone. © renewed 1981 by Monica Sone. By permission of Little, Brown and Company. Pp. 71, 73-74, 78-79.

p. 82: Reprinted by permission of the publisher from *Through Harsh Winters: The Life of a Japanese Immigrant Woman,* by Akemi Kikumura. Copyright © 1981 by Chandler & Sharp Publishers, Inc., Novato, Calif. All rights reserved. Page 92.

p. 83, top: Uchida, *Desert Exile,* 22.

p. 83, bottom: Reprinted by permission of the publisher from *Through Harsh Winters: The Life of a Japanese Immigrant Woman,* by Akemi Kikumura. Copyright © 1981 by Chandler & Sharp Publishers, Inc., Novato, Calif. All rights reserved. Pages 58-59.

p. 84: Uchida, *Desert Exile,* 17-19.

p. 85, top: Stanush, Barbara Evans, *Texans: A Story of Texan Cultures for Young People* (San Antonio: University of Texas Institute of Texan Cultures, 1988), 93-94.

p. 85, bottom: Rita Kasch Chegin, *Survivors: Women of the Southwest* (Las Cruces, N.M.: Yucca Tree Press, 1991), 118.

p. 86: Alice Murata, interview with Dorothy Hoobler, 1995.

p. 87: Amy Uno Ishii, interviewed by Betty E. Mitson and Kristin Mitchell, July 9, 1973, and July 20, 1973; California State University, Fullerton Oral History Program (O.H. 1342), pp. 5-6.

p. 88, top: Takaki, *A Different Mirror*, 266.

p. 88, bottom: Giles R. Wright with Howard L. Green and Lee R. Parks, *Schooling and Education* (Trenton: New Jersey Historical Commission, 1987), 29-30.

p. 89, top: Hazama and Komeiji, *Okage Sama De*, 241.

p. 89, bottom: From *Nisei Daughter* by Monica Sone. Copyright © 1953 by Monica Sone. © renewed 1981 by Monica Sone. By permission of Little, Brown and Company. Pp. 20, 22.

p. 90: Matsumoto, *Country Voices*, 141.

p. 91: Ito, *Issei*, 627-28.

p. 92, top: Saiki, *Japanese Women in Hawaii*, 82.

p. 92, bottom: Reprinted by permission of the publisher from *Through Harsh Winters: The Life of a Japanese Immigrant Woman*, by Akemi Kikumura. Copyright © 1981 by Chandler & Sharp Publishers, Inc., Novato, Calif. All rights reserved. Pages 79-80.

p. 93: Chegin, *Survivors*, 118-20.

p. 94, top: *Uchinanchu: A History of Okinawans in Hawaii*. Edited by Michi Kodama-Nishimoto and Mitsugu Sakihara. Published by Ethnic Studies Oral History Project (renamed the Center for Oral History in 1987), University of Hawaii at Manoa and the United Okinawan Association of Hawaii, Honolulu, 1981. Page 62.

p. 94, bottom: Uchida, *Desert Exile*, 31-35.

p. 96: *Hanahana: An Oral History Anthology of Hawaii's Working People*, by Michi Kodama-Nishimoto, Warren S. Nishimoto, and Cynthia A. Oshiro. Published by the Ethnic Studies Oral History Project (renamed the Center for Oral History in 1987), University of Hawaii at Manoa, Honolulu, 1984. Page 67.

p. 97, top: Mei T. Nakano, *Japanese American Women: Three Generations, 1890–1990* (Berkeley, Calif.: Mina Press, 1990), 127.

p. 97, middle: Matsumoto and Lerrigo, *A Brother Is A Stranger*, 212-13.

p. 97, bottom: Hosokawa, *Nisei*, 233.

p. 98, top: Namias, *First Generation*, 130-31.

p. 98, middle: Seichi Hayashida and Chiyeko Hayashida, interview, 9/7/89 (Boise: Idaho Oral History Center, 1989), 24-25.

p. 98, bottom: Charles Kikuchi, *The Kikuchi Diary: Chronicle from an American Concentration Camp*, ed. John Modell (Urbana: University of Illinois Press, 1973), 53-54.

p. 99: Hazama and Komeiji, *Okage Sama De*, 136.

p. 100, top: Leslie T. Hatamiya, *Righting a Wrong: Japanese Americans and the Passage of the Civil Rights Act of 1988* (Palo Alto: Stanford University Press, 1995), 95.

p. 100, bottom: Joann Faung Jean Lee, *Asian Americans: Oral Histories* (New York: The New Press, 1991), 14-15.

p. 101, top: Seichi Hayashida and Chiyeko Hayashida, interview, 9/7/89 (Boise: Idaho Oral History Center, 1989), 7-8, 19.

p. 101, bottom: Giles R. Wright, *Looking Back: Eleven Life Histories* (Trenton: New Jersey Historical Commission, 1986), 40-42.

p. 102: Excerpts from pp. 72-74 of *Farewell to Manzanar* by James D. and Jeanne Wakatsuki Houston. Copyright © 1973 by James D. Houston. Reprinted by permission of Houghton Mifflin Co. All rights reserved.

p. 103: Hosokawa, *Nisei*, 400-401.

p. 108, top: Uchida, *Desert Exile*, 149.

p. 108, middle: Wright, *Looking Back*, 42-44.

p. 108, bottom: Teddy Yoshikami, interview with Dorothy Hoobler, 1994.

p. 109, top: Seichi Hayashida and Chiyeko Hayashida, interview, 9/7/89 (Boise: Idaho Oral History Center, 1989), 25.

p. 109, bottom: *Hanahana: An Oral History Anthology of Hawaii's Working People*, by Michi Kodama-Nishimoto, Warren S. Nishimoto, and Cynthia A. Oshiro. Published by the Ethnic Studies Oral History Project (renamed the Center for Oral History in 1987), University of Hawaii at Manoa, Honolulu, 1984. Page 71.

p. 110, top: LaGumina and Cavaioli, *The Ethnic Dimension*, 118.

p. 110, bottom: Namias, *First Generation*, 78.

p. 111, top: Mary Motley Kalergis, *Home of the Brave* (New York: Dutton, 1989), unpaged.

p. 111, bottom: Uchida, *Desert Exile*, 147-48.

p. 112: Seichi Hayashida and Chiyeko Hayashida, interview, 9/7/89 (Boise: Idaho Oral History Center, 1989), 8-9.

p. 113 top: Excerpt from p. 140 of *Farewell to Manzanar* by James D. and Jeanne Wakatsuki Houston. Copyright © 1973 by James D. Houston. Reprinted by permission of Houghton Mifflin Co. All rights reserved.

p. 113, middle: Hatamiya, *Righting a Wrong*, 96.

p. 113, bottom: Lee, *Asian Americans*, 18.

p. 114, top: Wright, *Looking Back*, 44.

p. 114, bottom: Uchida, *Desert Exile*, 30-31.

p. 115, top: Janet Nomura Morey and Wendy Dunn, *Famous Asian Americans* (New York: Cobblehill, 1992), 79.

p. 115, middle: From *The Issei: Portrait of a Pioneer*, edited by Eileen Sunada Sarasohn. Copyright © 1983 by the Issei Oral History Project, Inc. Pacific Books, Publishers, Palo Alto, Calif. Page 275.

p. 115, bottom: Nakano, *Japanese American Women*, 221.

p. 116, top: Green and Parks, *What Is Ethnicity?*, 22.

p. 116, bottom: Asian Women United of California, ed., *Making Waves: An Anthology of Writings by and about Asian American Women* (Boston: Beacon Press, 1989), 143.

Sidebars

p. 13: Yuji Ichioka, *The Issei: The World of the First Generation Japanese Immigrants, 1885–1924* (New York: The Free Press, 1988), 45.

p. 15: Akemi Kikumura, *Issei Pioneers: Hawaii and the Mainland, 1885–1924* (Los Angeles: Japanese American National Museum, 1992), 64-65.

p. 19: Kikumura, *Issei Pioneers*, 58.

p. 21: Ichioka, *The Issei*, 61.

p. 25: Bill Hosokawa, *Nisei: The Quiet Americans* (Niwot: University Press of Colorado, 1992), 46.

p. 26: Dorothy Ochiai Hazama and Jane Okamoto Komeiji, *Okage Sama De: The Japanese in Hawaii, 1885–1985* (Honolulu: Bess Press, 1986), 15.

p. 30: From *The Issei: Portrait of a Pioneer*, edited by Eileen Sunada Sarasohn. Copyright © 1983 by the Issei Oral History Project, Inc. Pacific Books, Publishers, Palo Alto, Calif. Page 55.

p. 40: Hazama and Komeiji, *Okage Sama De*, 8.

p. 50: Franklin Odo and Kazuko Sinoto, *A Pictorial History of the Japanese in Hawai'i, 1885–1924* (Honolulu: Bishop Museum Press, 1985), 39-40, 45.

p. 57: Ichioka, *The Issei*, 26-27.

p. 58: Hosokawa, *Nisei*, 67.

p. 61: Ichioka, *The Issei*, 79.

p. 63: Hosokawa, *Nisei*, 82-83.

p. 77: Kazuo Ito, *Issei: A History of Japanese Immigrants in North America*, trans. Shinichiro Nakamura and Jean S. Gerard (Seattle: Japanese Community Service, 1973), 803.

p. 78: Kikumura, *Issei Pioneers*, 51.

p. 79: Hosokawa, *Nisei*, 200.

p. 93: Kikumura, *Issei Pioneers*, 67-68.

p. 94: Kikumura, *Issei Pioneers*, 69.

p. 96: Ronald Takaki, *A Different Mirror: A History of Multicultural America* (Boston: Little, Brown, 1993), 380.

p. 109: Hosokawa, *Nisei*, 414.

p. 110: Takaki, *A Different Mirror*, 400.

p. 117: Leslie T. Hatamiya, *Righting a Wrong: Japanese Americans and the Passage of the Civil Liberties Act of 1988* (Palo Alto: Stanford University Press, 1993), 190.

PICTURE CREDITS

Arizona Historical Foundation: 99 bottom; Balch Institute for Ethnic Studies: 10 (Iwata family collection), 11 (Iwata family collection), 14 bottom (Iwata family collection), 15 (Iwata family collection), 26 (Okamoto family collection), 108 bottom (Saburo and Michiyo Inouye collection), 110 (Sumiko Kobayashi collection), 116 top (Sumiko Kobayashi collection), 116 bottom (Nakai family collection); Bettmann Archive: 12 bottom; Bishop Museum: 22, 24 bottom, 28 (State Archives), 34 (Hedemann Collection), 48 top, 50 (R. J. Baker Collection), 51 bottom (Ray Jerome Baker), 52 bottom, 54, 78 right, 85 top (M. Koga), 89 bottom, 92; City Lore: 114 top; Denver Public Library, Western History Department: 44, 94 left; El Monte Historical Museum: cover, 66 bottom, 68 top, 69, 98 bottom, 102 bottom, 113 bottom; Folsom Historical Society Collection, City of Sacramento History and Science Division, Sacramento Archives and Museum Collection Center: 60 bottom; Hawai'i State Archives: 5, 35, 37, 40, 48 bottom, 51 top, 52 top, 53, 55, 56 top, 77, 78 left; courtesy of Hetzel Collection, Imperial County Historical Society: 65, 81 bottom, 90 bottom; Thomas and Dorothy Hoobler: 14 top, 16 bottom, 117 bottom; Idaho State Historical Society: 56 bottom (#78-2.90/i), 100 bottom (#76-29.1/mmm); courtesy of Senator Daniel Inouye, 103; Institute of Texan Cultures, San Antonio, Texas, courtesy of Julia May and Nina Onishi: 42, 64 bottom; Japanese American Citizens League, Chicago chapter: 27, 30, 46, 49, 66 top, 74, 79, 86 bottom, 89 top; Japanese American Citizens League, national headquarters: 80 bottom, 108 top; Japanese American History Archives: 31, 36 bottom, 38, 67 bottom, 70 top, 81 top, 106; Japanese American National Museum: 29 (courtesy of Tamura family), 43 top (courtesy of Y. Matsushima), 47 (courtesy of A. Dean), 58 (courtesy of Y. Matsushima), 59 top (courtesy of G. Nomura), 59 bottom (courtesy of A. Dean), 84 bottom (courtesy of R. Namba); Mary Koga: 117 top right; Bessie Miyeko (Yoshida) Konishi: 19; Library of Congress: 88; Millicent Library/Spinner Publications, Inc.: 20; Yasuo Mizuuchi: 117 middle; Morikami Museum: 43 bottom, 83 top; Dr. Alice Murata: 17, 24 top, 62 bottom, 63, 76 bottom, 87 bottom, 111 top, 111 bottom; Museum of Modern Art/Film Stills Archive: 6 bottom; National Archives: 13, 32, 36 top, 96 left, 97 bottom, 98 top, 99 top, 100 top, 101 top, 101 bottom, 102 top; National Aeronautics and Space Administration: 115; National Archives, Pacific Sierra Region: 39 top, 39 bottom; Shigeko Niizumi: 117 top left; Oregon Historical Society: frontispiece (#118G015), 82 top (#0069G056); courtesy of Bacon Sakatani: 72, 90 top; compliments of Seabrook Educational and Cultural Center: 16 top, 60 top, 75, 86 top, 87 top, 93, 104, 107, 109, 113 top, 114 bottom; Seattle Post-Intelligencer Collection, Museum of History and Industry, Seattle: 71, 96 right, 97 top; Security Pacific National Bank Photograph Collection, Los Angeles Public Library: 8, 82 bottom, 94 right; Sinclair Collection, Rutgers University: 21; courtesy of George Takei: 6 (all except bottom), 7; UPI/Bettmann: 64 top, 91; courtesy of Western Treasure Valley Cultural Center: 68 bottom (Yoshimi Yamamoto, donor), 76 top (Alice Nishitani, donor), 83 bottom (Alice Nishitani, donor), 84 top (Kay Maeda, donor), 85 bottom (Janet Koda, donor); Wing Luke Asian Museum: 61 (K. Norikane), 62 top (Ryo Tsai Collection), 80 top (K. Norikane), 95 (Betsuin Archives).

INDEX

ACKNOWLEDGMENTS

Many people generously gave their time, information, advice, memories, and photographs to produce this book. We owe a particular debt of gratitude to: Timothy K. Asamen of the Imperial Valley Historical Society; John N. Fuyuume, project director of the Seabrook Educational and Cultural Center; Ito Kazuo, who collected more than a thousand pages of firsthand recollections in his wonderful book, *Issei: A History of Japanese Immigrants in North America;* Michi Kodama-Nishimoto, research coordinator of the Center for Oral History at the University of Hawaii at Manoa; Marge Kemp of the Bishop Museum; Fred Love and Donna Crippen of the El Monte Historical Museum; Dr. Alice Murata, who shared her personal family album and recollections with us; Brian Niiya, Jennifer Mikami, and Akemi Kikumura of the Japanese American National Museum; Seizo Oka, executive director of the Japanese American History Archives; Mizue Sawano, our dear friend; Chiye Tomihiro of the Japanese American Citizens League, Chicago chapter; and Theodora Morita Yoshikami.

We also wish to acknowledge the valuable and generous help we received from James Allen of the Arizona Historical Foundation; Andrea Ambrose of the Fresno Metropolitan Museum; Diane Bruce of the Institute of Texan Cultures; Rick Caldwell of the Museum of History and Industry, Seattle; Carolyn Cole of the Los Angeles Public Library; Tara Deal and Nancy Toff, our inexhaustible editors at Oxford University Press; Katherine Child Debs, curator of the Western Treasure Valley Cultural Center; Gail E. Farr of the Balch Institute for Ethnic Studies; Tom Gregersen of the Morikami Museum; Art Hansen, director of the oral history program at California State University at Fullerton; Bill Hosokawa; Senator Daniel Inouye; Linda Morton Keithley of the Idaho State Historical Society; Mary Koga; Waverly Lowell of the National Archives, Pacific Sierra Region; June Namias; Masi Nihei and Emily A. Nishi of the Japanese American Citizens League; Charlene Noyes of the City of Sacramento History and Science Division; Carl Ruberg of the Ellis Island Immigration Museum; Bacon Sakatani; Kathey Swan of the Denver Public Library; Mikki Tint of the Oregon Historical Society; Dr. Clifford Uyeda, president of the National Japanese American Historical Society; and Ruth Vincent of the Wing Luke Asian Museum.

Finally, we were honored by the kindness of Ken Kawaichi and Susan Tamura, who opened their own Japanese American family album and shared with us their memories of family members past and present. To them, and to everyone else, *okage sama de.*

ABOUT THE AUTHORS

Dorothy and Thomas Hoobler have published more than 50 books for children and young adults, including *Margaret Mead: A Life in Science; Vietnam: Why We Fought; Showa: The Age of Hirohito; Buddhism;* and *Japanese Portraits.* Their works have been honored by the Society for School Librarians International, the Library of Congress, the New York Public Library, the National Council for Social Studies, and *Best Books for Children,* among other organizations and publications. The Hooblers have also written several volumes of historical fiction for children, including *Next Stop Freedom, Frontier Diary, The Summer of Dreams,* and *Treasure in the Stream.* Dorothy Hoobler received her master's degree in American history from New York University and worked as a textbook editor before becoming a full-time free-lance editor and writer. Thomas Hoobler received his master's degree in education from Xavier University and has worked as a teacher and textbook editor.

306.8

DATE DU

306.8
Hoo

Hoobler, Dorothy.

The Japanese American
family album

16 105

DATE DUE	BORROWER'S NAME	ROOM NUMBER

306.8
Hoo

Hoobler, Dorothy.

The Japanese American
family album